EMBRACING LEADERSHIFT

Extraordinary Results Through Enhanced Communication and Collaboration

Ricardo Lopes

10-10-10
Publishing

EMBRACING LEADERSHIFT
Extraordinary Results Through Enhanced Communication and Collaboration
Five Steps to Influence and Inspire Extraordinary Results™
www.embracingleadershift.com

Publisher
10-10-10 Publishing
Markham, ON   Canada

Printed in Canada and the United States of America

TABLE OF CONTENTS

In memory of my parents, Maria José and Agostinho Lopes, who left this world long before I could adequately thank them for their commitment to their family, and long before I could grasp the depth of their exemplary leadership in fairness, genuineness, and compassion for others.

To my better half, Zelia, whose support and quiet strength have been unwavering.

To my daughter, Jillian, whose support and contributions affirm that God blesses some of us with talent, discipline, and commitment to excellence beyond our years.

To my son, Christian, whose patience and compassion inspire me every day.

Finally, to my sister, Anna, who has been my lifelong cheerleader.

"You have not lived today until you have done something for someone who can never repay you."

– John Bunyan (Puritan preacher and the English author of *The Pilgrim's Progress*)

"Surround yourself only with people who are going to take you higher."

– Oprah Winfrey (American media executive, actress, talk show host, television producer, and philanthropist. North America's first black multi-billionaire, and the greatest black philanthropist in American history)

Foreword

Would you like to transform your business, the team you lead, or the team you collaborate with, and achieve extraordinary results? The demand for 'soft skills' that help you bridge differences in culture, values, commitments to learning etc., and lead a team to success, have never been more important, as organizations restructure, temporary workforces continue to grow, operations move overseas, and the diversity of team members themselves continues to grow. *EMBRACING LEADERSHIFT: Extraordinary Results Through Enhanced Communication and Collaboration* highlights some of these trends in businesses today, the challenges, as well as opportunities, that you may be experiencing when it comes to generating results with diverse people who think, act, value, are motivated, or aspire to be, do, or have, differently.

The days of "command and control" where your workforce will do as they are told, or contribute in an extraordinary way because of your title, are coming to an end. Today your ability to generate results and extract someone's "discretionary effort" is dependent on your ability to persuade them, to influence them, to inspire them, to engage with another, in some extraordinary way. It's not surprising that earlier this year, LinkedIn's CEO Jeff Weiner reported the biggest skill gaps on résumés today aren't hard skills like coding etc., but instead are gaps in the soft skills: communication, team-building and leadership. These are the skills that you need, in order to pull out the very best in your diverse teams, who have different experiences, backgrounds, and ideas on how to solve problems by leveraging creativity and innovation. This is the blessing of diversity over teams of sameness, but it also demands more from you, as the leader of your team or as an individual leader and subject matter expert working with your collaborating peers. You must be able to influence and inspire others to generate results with care and genuineness. This is crucial, if you expect to see contributions of effort beyond what keeps your team members employed. If 'ordinary team results' have never really been your thing, and you prefer 'extraordinary' on anything that has your name on it, it's going to require some extraordinary leadership skills.

It won't take you too long to realize Ricardo is passionate about leadership, and about helping you meet with success. Ricardo's research from experts in their respective fields of neuroscience, change management, leadership etc. will help you see what most are missing. Ricardo's *Five Steps to Influence and Inspire Extraordinary Results*™ is a powerful engagement process that you, as a leader of a team or as an individual leader among collaborating peers, can use to bridge 'generation gaps', 'cultural gaps', 'familiarity gaps' etc. and achieve extraordinary results. Having led teams to extraordinary himself for decades, Ricardo knows a thing or two about motivating others to extraordinary results. But this book is more than just a book of tips and tricks. This book came together as a result of Ricardo's unrelenting curiosity around questions like: What do industry leaders do to bring out the very best in their teams and achieve results that consistently surpass competitor results, despite economic conditions, technological advancements etc.? Why do some methods work, while others do not? Does the scientific community provide clues as to why some processes are more successful than others?

I hope the research, implementation examples, and the impressive results of those who have adopted many of these practices inspires you. I encourage you to use the 'reflection pages' to make notes and chart your own plan for achieving extraordinary results when working with others. Don't add this book to your "shelf-help" library of dusty books with valuable insights that never get implemented. *EMBRACING LEADERSHIFT: Extraordinary Results*

Through Enhanced Communication and Collaboration does more than just provide you with more information; it provides you with the means to transformation.

Raymond Aaron
New York Times Bestselling Author

Chapter One

Introduction: Disruptive Changes

"The marriage of computing and connectivity without the shackles of being tethered to a location is one of the biggest disruptive forces of modern times."
– Om Malik (Indian-American web and technology writer, and True Ventures partner)

"Without change, there is no innovation, creativity, or incentive for improvement. Those who initiate change will have a better opportunity to manage the change that is inevitable."
– William Pollard (English clergyman and writer)

Call to Action and My Wish for You

"As a leader, the first person I need to lead is me.
The first person that I should try to change is me."
– John C. Maxwell (American *New York Times* bestselling author, speaker, pastor, and internationally recognized leadership and management development expert)

You're busy, and if you're anything like I was for the bulk of my professional career, you looked after others first, at work and at home. You gave to and supported everyone else before you looked to supporting your own personal development, and your list of "one day I'll do this or that for myself" is getting longer and longer. You may be cranking out the results, and celebrating win after win, following a quasi-school of hard knocks and a haphazard personal development formula that has worked for you and generated *success*. You may have adopted, and may even wear, the slogan, "Hustle." You pride yourself on the commitment and effort you put forth to create results, while putting work before other causes and other people who would appreciate more of your presence, and you of theirs. You may be so busy that you rarely look to improve yourself, and any information that you are exposed to, which promises to enhance your ability to influence and inspire others, quickly dissipates. Research tells us that adult learners forget 87% of any learned content within 90 days, if the work isn't done to incorporate new learning into existing patterns of thought, speech, and behaviour. The work waiting for you back at the office, after your little *training getaway*, discourages you from taking the time to review your material, or to think of systems to incorporate the content, or to seek the help you need in order to integrate new learning in the form of a coach or implementation partner, who holds your focus and holds you accountable. You may not even know it, but you're missing out on something.

I spent two years researching this book. I didn't want it to be a list of anecdotal recommendations whose value would be measured against my personal past performances. I had some great wins in chasing sales targets, customer satisfaction indexes, and employee satisfaction scores, and I could have done it all so much better! I read book after book, interviewed leaders in several industries, read research paper after research paper, attended conferences in and out of the country, went to the United States and studied with one of the top internationally recognized leadership and management development experts, John C. Maxwell, and hired multiple coaches and mentors to help grow my skills and my business. If you know me, you'd think I was overcome with feelings of joy and satisfaction, given that I love to learn and I love to teach, and one passion informs the other. But I wasn't happy or joyful; in fact, I experienced anger, resentment, and regret. You see, had I been exposed to this research twenty years earlier, I could have done so much better, with far less effort, and I wouldn't have had to sacrifice time spent with people or doing more of the things I wanted to do. Today, people are telling you and your children that "in order to be successful, you need to 'hustle' and work 50–60 hours a week. Forget about work-life balance; you may even have to sleep here." But don't believe it. The truth is, as the leader of a team, or as an individual leader among collaborating peers, you can achieve extraordinary results and work-life balance, leveraging content that most people are clueless about. If you invest the time to get through this book, you'll probably be left wondering, as do I, why more organizations and individuals haven't tapped into more of these truths, to generate extraordinary results like so many before them.

Sharing knowledge and empowering others has always been a passion for me. This is my genuine, well-intending invitation and call to action for you. Do yourself a favor: stop, and clear a couple of days to read through this book. Doing so will bring clarity to processes and truths that your experiences and your intuition will tell you are effective when influencing and inspiring others to extraordinary results. Read through this book, and find out why what is working works, and why what trips you up is tripping you up without you knowing why. Like me, I suspect you will shout out, "That's why that worked so well," or, "Damn, I dropped the ball there." Use the reflection pages* at the end of each chapter, describing the *Five Steps to Influence and Inspire Extraordinary Results*™, to jot down ideas you want to implement, and create little action plans to ensure you are incorporating new insights into your existing patterns of thought, speech, and behaviour. Otherwise, the content in this book, like other powerful books before it, become what I call *shelf-help resources*, which offer great insights into improving oneself, yet they collect dust on shelves as they were read more for *enter-train-ment* value than development.

*If you prefer to work on digital expanding "Reflection Pages" to summarize and plan your skills implementation strategy, you can get the document at www.embracingleadershift.com where you can access this tool and several other exclusive book bonus materials.

I never had such a resource myself, and I never appreciated the uniqueness and importance of each step in the leader's engagement process described below. Now I do, and I hope you will too. At a time when working environments change at a predictable never-before-seen pace, due to the accelerant technology, so too do the skills required to empower your success. If you stay where you are, you will undoubtedly fall behind as your effectiveness is hindered by your reluctance to adapt to an ever-changing, more collaborative world where, at least for now, influencing and inspiring others to adopt new mindsets, exercise creativity, share information, and take action dominates. You are just as important as anything else currently on the go. Invest in yourself for the sake of your own *extraordinary* success, and in so doing, watch as your new strength empowers the *extraordinary* success of those around you. My wish for you is that you do the work, and in six months from now, even you will be surprised by your ability to influence, inspire, and generate extraordinary results.

How This Book Will Support You

This book will support you as the leader of a team or as an individual leader among collaborating peers, with the leadership tools you need in order to demonstrate enhanced communication that better influences, inspires, and generates extraordinary results. Whether your collaborators are local or international, physically present or remotely situated, culture sharing or diversity embracing, this book will explore each trend and the resulting need for enhanced *soft skills* to generate extraordinary success. Together, we will explore a leader's engagement process—*Five Steps to Influence and Inspire Extraordinary Results*™—based on decades of management experience and powerful insights from acclaimed researchers in the areas of change management, neuroscience, behavioural science, data management, economics, psychology, leadership development, and management development. This leader's engagement process provides a structure and guidance that a leader can use to identify and acknowledge the uniqueness of diverse individuals with whom they are collaborating. It is this individualized attention to detail, and demonstration of genuine care, that empowers a leader's ability to influence and inspire others to extraordinary results. The *Five Steps to Influence and Inspire Extraordinary Results*™ have repeatable steps, including: Making a Connection, Building Relationships, Establishing Trust, Casting a Vision, and Creating Buy-in. You cannot skip a step or stop halfway through them and still expect to generate extraordinary results. What you discover about individuals along the way, and what learnings you leverage to influence and inspire, will vary, as do the individuals you are collaborating with, but the process remains the same.

It took considerable effort to amalgamate vast amounts of research into *Five Steps to Influence and Inspire Extraordinary Results*™. Some of the processes capitalize on new research in neuroscience about the inner workings of the human brain and how it processes information while making decisions. This knowledge has only more recently been used in marketing, to influence and inspire consumer behaviour. Some have likened leveraging the inner workings of the human brain as unethical, and have lobbied to have the practice banned, much like subliminal advertising. It hasn't been banned in the marketing world, yet. Like any powerful tool, be it atomic energy, a smart phone, or the internet, whether it produces good or bad depends on who holds it. We'll look at studies that highlight why the employee engagement percentage is in the 70s at certain organizations who share select attributes, while the global average is only 15%, and the American/Canadian average is 31%[1]. We'll see what organizations, like 3M, Sony, Proctor and Gamble, Disney, Johnson and Johnson, and Hewlett-Packard, do to influence and inspire their employees, and subsequently outperform their competition in the marketplace by a factor of 12, since 1925. These organizations aren't satisfied with *successful;* they reach for *extraordinary,* and they have successfully achieved this over decades of changing times—changes that at the time were every bit as dramatic as some of the changes we are witnessing today. Let's look at a few examples of change we are experiencing now, which is affecting working dynamics and what it takes to be successful today.

Accelerated Change

We're witnessing a transformation in workplace technology, project methodology, transient workforces, organizational hierarchies, diversity in global business partnerships, as well as increased diversity in the people within departments themselves. You may find yourself working in a far more collaborative environment, and quickly learning that you too must adapt and evolve in order to be successful and remain relevant. If you work in a larger company, you have no doubt witnessed dramatic changes in the last few years with respect to the physical space, technologies, number of people sitting (or standing) alongside you, etc. You have probably heard many titans, like Henry Ford, proclaim, "Never before have we seen such accelerated change due to technology as we are witnessing today." The statement still rings as true today as it did 100 years ago.

New Spaces and New Faces

Organizations are evolving to implement quick changes in a race to increase profits via expense optimization, improved efficiencies, and enhancements to the customer experience, to get ahead of the competition. Workers are coming back to, or joining, newly restructured teams that may or may not be physically present, or even in the same country. Some of the newer faces are working their next gig and merely passing through. Many employees are arriving to freshly painted, open concept, ecosystem environments, with enhanced technology and communal work spaces, finding themselves having to adapt quickly, or fail. However, reorganizing groups of individuals is trickier than switching out the telephone system. Along with changes to position charts comes changes in group dynamics, relationships, legacy knowledge, and project momentum. Regardless, employees are expected to perform effectively as more independent, highly skilled subject matter experts, in far more collaborative environments.

The Shift in Leadership and the Growth in Collaboration

Individual Leadership

The *shift* in *leadership* comes as leaders borrowing authority from a hierarchy are replaced by agile networks of subject matter experts working in collaborative teams, where each collaborator takes turns playing the role of *leader* as they share their knowledge and unique contribution to the team's effort. In these environments, your success, and the project's success, is dependent on your *individual leadership*; that is, your ability to influence and inspire the mindset and behavior of others in a collaboration, while ensuring that both individual mandates and collective project requirements are met.

Team Leaders

We still have team leaders, of course, overseeing collaborating teams and the more traditional hierarchy-based teams. The manager's skill in each case is becoming more and more important to the creativity and productivity of the team. Hence, the team's lead role is changing too. The days of command and control are ending. Workers aren't influenced or inspired to action based on the leadership expressed in your title, but rather the leadership expressed in your patterns of thought, speech, and behavior. With the rapid changes and expansion in processes, technologies, global markets, etc., leaders can no longer know everything, nor are they expected to. Successful leaders surround themselves with smart people who have access to the answers, then work hard to influence, inspire, challenge, motivate, and empower their teams to perform the tasks that serve the current mission and the longer-term organizational vision. To get the best out of their employees, "performance management systems are more orientated around basic human needs for psychological engagement, such as positive workplace relationships, frequent recognition, ongoing performance conversations and opportunities for personal development." [2] Managers don't give feedback just in performance appraisals anymore; employees want more frequent feedback and regular goal setting in an open collaborative process. Evaluations pull data from increasingly robust data sources, so the manager role is moving from a performance evaluating function, to one more focused on coaching and developing people. [3]

Leader Readiness

But how ready are leaders to influence and inspire with new patterns of thought, speech, and behavior that generate extraordinary results in an evolving workforce?

Gallup has been studying individual and managerial talents and trends for five decades. In their "State of the American Manager: Analytics and Advice for Leaders" research, they reveal that only 1 in 10 managers are naturally suited to be managers and another 2 in 10 managers "exhibit some characteristics of basic managerial talent." [4]

Leadership development has been a consistent area of concern for decades, with Deloitte reporting in its Human Capital Trends Survey that Canadian CEOs and senior HR professionals identified leadership capability as its most important and pressing challenge. [5]

Brandon Hall Group's research extended across 32 counties and 27 industries, and found that a deficit in leaders with high-quality skills is a global concern. They found that leadership development earned a top spot in organization's talent priority lists, as 71 percent of organizations said "their leaders are not ready to lead their organization into the future... Proactively managing leaders' skill gaps was the number one reason cited as a critical priority for improving leadership development by 57% of those organizations." And the skills of coaching, communication, and collaboration were among the top five skills listed as having significant gaps. [6] Such gaps in leadership skills are troublesome, given their contributions to uninspired workforces and lost business opportunities.

Is Leadership Important?

After studying 2.5 million manager-led teams, in 195 countries, Gallup reported that *talented managers* were found to "frequently realize 48 percent greater profitability, 22 percent greater productivity, 17 percent greater employee engagement, 5 percent greater customer engagement, and 19 percent less turnover." [7] Among the best-managed companies in Gallup's database, as many as 70% of employees are engaged at work, compared to a worldwide average of a mere 15%, and 31% in Canada/U.S. The best managed companies in the top quartile of Gallop's database generated 17% more productivity, and 21% more profit than those in the bottom quartile. [8] According to Gallup, engaged employees are adults working full time for an employer, who are highly involved and are enthusiastic about their work and workplace. There are many things an organization can do to encourage employee engagement, but Gallup finds that "managers account for at least 70% of the variance in employee engagement scores across business units." [9] This is an inspiring statistic, and an incredible opportunity, but it isn't new.

Research done by the Wilson Learning Corporation, and reported in The Study of Business Performance, Employee Satisfaction, and Leadership, reported two decades ago that "69 percent of the variability in personal satisfaction was attributable to the quality of employee's relationship with their managers," and stated, "39% of variability in corporate performance is attributable to the personal satisfaction of the employees." [10]

For decades, we have seen the connection between employees' picks for "Best Places to Work," and shareholder returns, reduced turnover, better customer satisfaction, etc. For example, organizations named in the "Fortune 100 Best Companies to Work For" list, have consistently produced over 40% more in financial performance (almost 2:1) than their peers in the market, for over 20 years. [11]

Clearly, leadership consistently drives employee performance and satisfaction metrics that subsequently drive performance metrics. So, what do leaders have to do to influence and inspire employees to achieve extraordinary results? Is it the team building events, the CEO's annual message to employees, or the ping pong tables, free swag, and popcorn that leaders provide that makes the difference? Is it a leader's ability to tap into an employee's needs for physical, mental, emotional, and spiritual health? Is this what spawned the rise in work-life balance, commitment to personal development, commitments to offer personal recognition more frequently, or the increased focus on working with a sense of purpose? All of these are important, in different measures, to different employees, and so the responsibility lies with the leader to best determine what influences and inspires others to extraordinary results.

We are obsessed with putting people into categories and boxes, where no one person fits perfectly. Millennials are an obvious example, and given that they are currently the largest generational cohort currently in the workforce, the size of which we haven't seen since the post war baby boomers, they get a lot of attention. I'm always amazed by finger pointers who judge them harshly. They are doing what we all did when we started a career and were looking to build a portfolio of skills and improve our earning potential in preparation to build a life, home, and family that suited our preferences. We speak to their preference for learning, and compare the species in its habitat to others like baby boomers who currently want considerably less training. Of course, baby boomers are starting to visualize their retirement, have years of cultivated skills, and many are at the peak of their historical earning power. One day, much of the published content about millennials will become obsolete, because so many were focused on labelling and cataloguing the surface behaviours of the generation, as opposed to making the effort to understand what these individuals needed in their life at the time. As the research below will show, millennials move frequently because, when their leadership skills that have become very important in today's workplace are not being developed, they feel that they *have to*. Their actions are not driven by a compromised sense of loyalty but rather out of practical necessity and admirable desire to achieve. In fact, the research demonstrates that millennial retention goes up at organizations where development and encouraging young people into leadership roles exists.

Often, those who lack the leadership skills that are required to tap into the uniqueness of those they aim to influence and inspire, make up stories, and they say that people are not loyal, and that they are entitled, lazy, etc., because they don't know how to close the *gap* in communication and understanding. As a leader of a team or as an individual leader among collaborating peers, you need to take the time to understand what influences and inspires others to extraordinary results, on a case by case basis. There is no easy one-size, one-action-fits-all strategy, where once implemented, influences and inspires everyone to stardom. Fortunately, in chapter 4, I propose a consistent process you can use to acknowledge an individual's uniqueness, and demonstrate genuine care, while effectively influencing and inspiring extraordinary results. Leaders like you are challenged to elicit performance, and if you aspire to achieve *extraordinary performance*, you need to be able to elicit *extraordinary employee contributions or discretionary effort* that exceeds what is contractually required of them.

Opportunities in Scaling Leadership

The research to date has studied the leading manager's performance in *manager-led teams*. Imagine where engagement, satisfaction, creativity, effectiveness, etc. could go, given the *shift in leadership*. There can now be several more formally recognized *individual leaders* on collaborating teams, and a team manager or *leader*, each contributing at higher levels of leadership competency in communication and collaboration. What if almost everyone knows how to influence, inspire, and generate extraordinary results from others while working in collaborations? What would employee engagement at work look like or feel like when everyone has your back and is growing together? What kind of extraordinary business results would come to be, given the escalating employee engagement, satisfaction, creativity, collaboration, etc.? This is exciting to think about, and a little scary. It's possible that the additional presence of leaders, and the subsequent multiplier effect, would take the organization working in collaborative teams to new heights in business results. It's also possible to go the other way. If the masses are playing a significant motivating role in the professional lives of others, their lack of ability to influence and inspire might mean that they aren't able to elicit significant contributions in a collaboration. They could also be damaging employee engagement, satisfaction, etc. along the way, thus hampering the organization's business results. But with everyone on board, and done right, this is an opportunity to scale extraordinary. Newly evolved working dynamics afford opportunities today that previous successful businesses didn't have access to. Leaders of teams and individual leaders among collaborating peers, have a trailblazing occasion to take the lead, by working together to leverage their leadership skills in communication and collaboration, and support the creation of something extraordinary.

It will be interesting to study the relationship between employee engagement, satisfaction, etc., and business results in the coming years. Will leadership be redefined to include an evolving collaborative workforce, who each take turns playing the role of *leader,* as their unique subject matter expertise takes center stage in collaborations? It would appear that there's no getting around competency in leadership skill and its impact on positive business results, both in traditional hierarchical teams led by *a leader*, or in collaborating teams of *individual leaders.*

Leadership Is Influence and a Non-Negotiable New Standard

At a time when processes and technologies are being optimized to automate redundant tasks to computers, the learning and development focus has moved to the soft skills or the more human aspects of work. Current estimates for the half-life of *hard skills* are about 5 years, and they're declining quickly as tools, systems, software, and processes, etc. are continuously enhanced or replaced. But *soft skills,* like the leadership skills of being able to influence, inspire, and generate extraordinary results with your team or collaborating peers, are skills for life.

One of the world's top internationally recognized leadership and management experts, John C. Maxwell, teaches to no less than 21 different aspects of leadership. However, Maxwell summarizes, "Leadership is influence, nothing more and nothing less." At one time, individual leadership was a mark of distinction, a variant that signalled great potential to take on larger missions and opportunities to contribute in some extraordinary way. Today, individual leadership skills are the standard for the masses working in effective collaborative environments, and they're non-negotiable. The success of workers in collaborative teams, and the success of initiatives they *hustle* to advance, depend far more on the worker's ability to influence others, based on their leadership skills, than from any position of authority. Unfortunately, research findings repeatedly identify gaps in these skills and in leader readiness.

Training and Development – The Most Attractive Employee Benefit

Training has taken on increased importance in the workplace. LinkedIn, whose parent company is Microsoft, is a professional networking platform, having 610 million registered members in 200 counties around the world. LinkedIn polled talent developers, people managers, and executives regarding the most important skills for employees to learn in preparation for the future workplace. Is it any wonder that in their 2018 Workplace Learning Report, LinkedIn found that the top recommended priorities for learning and development programs were: 1) Leadership, 2) Communication, and 3) Collaboration.[12] Not only do organizations find these skills important, employees do too, and they're eager to learn them. Research done by Google, Gallup, and Deloitte finds training and the development of skills that support career progression in this evolved workplace, to be the most important benefits employees are looking for. In fact, training and development were ranked to be of far greater importance than free food, the likes of ping pong tables, the sharing of corporate values, or even health insurance. The millennial generation is the current dominating demographic cohort in today's workforce by numbers. They are at the stage in their careers where, like generations before them, they are working hard to build their careers and earning potential. If they don't see their employer's commitment to their development as leaders, they're leaving. In their 2016 Millennial Survey, Deloitte reported that an incredible 66% of millennials expect to leave their employer by 2020. They found that "71 percent of those likely to leave in the next two years are unhappy with how their leadership skills are being developed." Employees that did show greater loyalty to the organization were also more likely to agree that "there is a lot of support/training available to those wishing to take on leadership roles," and that "younger employees are actively encouraged to aim for leadership roles." [13]

The traditional advancing career path through promotions, after completing level after level in an upward climb of increasing complexity and responsibility, has been replaced, with advancement via a career path that evidences skills acquired via varying assignments, diverse experiences, and exposure to leadership assignments. Individuals used to train and get qualified for a job or function; now the job or career *is the training ground* as *change and learning are continuous.*

Learning and development teams at progressive organizations know this, and they are adopting different programs to create environments of learning, supporting employee mobility between roles, and have become *curators* of training content as opposed to the traditional *creators* of training content.[14] People managers and executives also know that getting employees to make time for learning is their number one challenge for talent development, and their number two challenge is getting managers involved in employee learning.[15] This is problematic as organizations work to hang on to their best talent, who are ready to leave if the organization doesn't support their development. LinkedIn's 2018 Workplace Learning Report indicates that "94% of employees would stay at a company longer if it invested in their career." Unfortunately, employees indicate that the "#1 reason employees feel held back from learning is because they don't have the time."[16]

Learning as a Priority

Learning, especially leadership capacity, is not about acquiring information; it's about supporting a transformation. This takes time, requires continuous effort, needs to cater to individual learning preferences, and mandates learning new content with supported implementation. This doesn't happen after merely watching a 20-minute online video. High-engagement companies know this, with executives spending money on learning, regularly meeting with teams and providing feedback, and genuinely caring about each individual's progress. In fact, "research on high-impact learning organizations, conducted in 2005, 2008, and 2011 [before, during, and after the last recession], showed each year that companies that 'overinvest' in L&D (spending per employee) rated highest in employee retention, innovation, and customer service, and outperformed their peers threefold in long-term profitability. This trend shows that investment in people matters during good times and bad." [17]

It's not enough to design new organizational charts and fill boxes with highly-skilled people who lack the enhanced mindset, communication, and behavioural skills to participate fully in these evolving workplaces. Learning and development programs, and individuals not supported by a learning and development department, need to ensure they invest in their workforce or themselves to empower their success in new environments, where hard skills and smarts don't guarantee success. As the CEO of LinkedIn, Jeff Weiner, announced in 2019, the greatest global skill gap identified in résumés today isn't *hard skills*; instead, it's the absence of *soft skills*, like communication, team-building, and leadership skills. Such skills in the leader of a team or in an individual leader among collaborating peers, can mean the difference between labored ordinary results, and extraordinary results that are achieved while maintaining a work-life balance.

Let's look at some examples of disruptive changes that present opportunities and challenges to reward and test a new kind of leader.

*Visit www.embracingleadershift.com for access to digital "Reflection Pages" and other exclusive book bonus materials available to you.

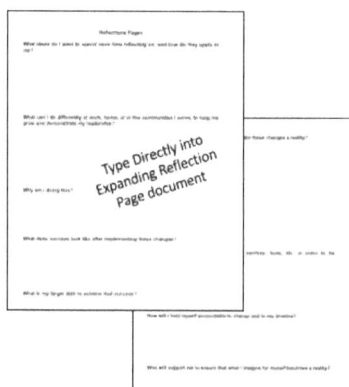

Notes:

1   Clifton, J. From the Chairman and CEO, Executive Summary - State of the Global Workplace, gallup.com; 2017
2   Ibid.
3   Beck R. and Harter J. Why Great Managers Are SO Rare. gallup.com; 2016
4   Ibid.
5   Stockton H, Pastakia K. Deloitte Perspectives Leadership development: a top concern in Canada deloitte.com
6   Loew L. STUDY SHOWS LEADERSHIP DEVELOPMENT RATED BELOW AVERAGE OR POOR IN MORE THAN ONE-THIRD OF ORGANIZATIONS. Trainingmag.com; 2015
7   Rigoni B, Baily N. Leadership Mistake: Promoting Based on Tenure. News.gallup.com; 2015
8   Bersin J, McDowell T, Rahnema A, Van Durme Y. The organization of the future arriving now. deloite.com; 2017.
9   Beck R. and Harter J. Why Great Managers Are SO Rare. gallup.com; 2016
10 Barrett R. Why the future belongs to value added companies. The Journal for Quality and Participation Vol. 22 Cincinnati; 1999.
11 Yoshimoto C, Frauenheim E. The Best Companies to Work For Are Beating the Market. Fortune.com; 2018.
12 Learning with Lynda.com content. 2018 Workplace Learning Report: The Rise and Responsibility of Talent Development in the New Labor Market. LinkedIn.com; 2018.
13 Deloitte's Millennial Survey 2016 executive summary. deloitte.com; 2016.
14 Pelster B, Johnson D, Stempel J, Van Der Vyver B. Deloitte – Careers and Learning: Realtime, all the time. 2017 Global Human Capital Trends. deloitte.com; 2017.
15 Learning with Lynda.com content. 2018 Workplace Learning Report: The Rise and Responsibility of Talent Development in the New Labor Market. LinkedIn.com; 2018.
16 Ibid.

17 Bersin J, Becoming irresistible: A new model for employee engagement – Deloitte -Review Issue 16. deloitte.com; 2015

Chapter Two

The Move to Individual Leaders
on Collaborating Teams

"None of us is as smart as all of us."
– Ken Blanchard (management expert and American author of
The One Minute Manager)

"Alone we can do so little; together we can do so much."
– Helen Keller (American author and political activist, and
first deaf-blind person to earn a Bachelor of Arts degree)

Changing *Workspaces*

Working dynamics have changed in part due to the adoption of remote-friendly collaborating technologies, allowing for tele-commuting, international partners, and the inclusion of a more transient workforce. Structural changes include the adoption of project methodologies like "Lean" or "Agile" leveraged in more communal working environments, and the flattening of organizations which has changed how many organizations get things done. The culture in these spaces is also in transition. More and more, behaviour guided by fear and the judgment of others is replaced with a culture that encourages risk-taking that is safe from judgment, in support of quick progress. The physical environments that workers occupy are changing too. Some of the changes include open space environments or ecologies having communal desks or meeting areas, laptops with VOIP phone service and central electronic file storage in favor of walls, personal desks, land lines, and personal files. These new environments incorporate a variety of meeting spaces, from "war rooms" where teams gather to strategize and move initiatives forward, to greenery infused Zen-like spaces, with inspiring views into the city that promote peace and rejuvenation. New technologies and physical environments have allowed for the adoption of different methods of generating results that are less top down managed via strict processes, and instead, are more collaborative and people centric. These people centric processes demand *people skills* or *soft skills,* which are required in order to effectively collaborate. In these environments, teams are made up of highly skilled subject matter experts strategically selected or self-organized, based on their valuable *hard skill* contributions to the initiative. But having the subject knowledge or hard skills, and not having the ability to influence the mindset or behaviour of those around you, won't help you or the initiative. New spaces and the resulting change to working relationship dynamics demand new skills.

The following are some examples where structural changes and technology have made dramatic changes in working environments, which now demand that individuals demonstrate leadership skills in order to effectively influence, inspire, and generate extraordinary results while working in more collaborative environments.

Agile – The Pressure to Communicate Effectively in an Agile Sprint

A 2017 McKinsey global survey revealed that two-thirds of respondents indicated that their companies had already begun agile transformations[1] and the corresponding disruption. The word, *disruption*, has been adopted to mean both the upset or disarrangement of the status quo, but also the promise of greater efficiencies in production, profitability, better alignment between solutions and coveted customer features, etc. Gone are the days of aiming for perfect execution and the perfect customer experience in favor of quick releases that serve majorities. With this mode of operation comes the acknowledgement that releases will require tweaking as users identify hiccups in the latest release.

Agile Benefits

Agile methodology has many benefits, including developing products that best suit the customer, are better aligned to the current market, and safeguards against guesswork and expensive development effort that never gets implemented, etc.

Agile Challenges

This movement has come with some challenges. While the *agile team*, for example, organizes strategic development moves in a flurry of colored post-it notes across walls that look like a battle field's aerial view, elsewhere in the organization, the battles are very real ones. While agile development plans show great promise, many larger organizations are hindered by legacy processes or less than agile systems that weren't designed to move as swiftly. Safety checks, requiring multiple eyes, levels of authorization prior to making changes within the organization, budgets assigned to different departments, ownership issues requiring negotiation, etc., all slow accelerated evolution. There will be years of process and system upgrades before larger organizations can move as quickly as colored post-it notes in the agile *war room*.

Enhanced Communication Skills Required

New methodologies have encouraged new ways of planning, execution, and communication. In an agile environment, teams work together in blocks of time, usually one to four-week periods, called a *sprint*. There may be disagreements within the team as to whether or not the development to software or systems is satisfactory, but when the time is up, development stops, and the team moves to another part of the project. Teams of motivated, talented developers and business people are trusted to work together and use face-to-face communication to transfer information. The flow is not the traditional process-centric; it's people-centric, where the focus is more on individuals and interactions, rather than on processes and the tools they use. This is a critical change where solid individual leadership skills become important, as strong communication and persuasion skills among collaborating team members are required to meet deadlines within a pressure building timed sprint. The management style also changes from command and control, to leadership and collaboration, where focus is placed on motivating people by creating an environment of appreciation, trust, and empowerment. While traditional processes and tools have been replaced by people-centric interactions, many say that the effectiveness of interactions are predominantly positive but still evolving.

Lean – Transparent Communication Supporting the Move to Leaner Operations

The successful implementation of this method relies on team collaboration and the adoption of a long-term mindset or culture committed to waste minimization. In lean environments, it's acceptable to change or fix processes only to have to revisit them again. Fixing it, fixing it again, and then fixing it yet again, is not unusual until improvements to value streams are optimized.

Lean Benefits

In lean environments, the goal is to provide perfect value to the customer through a perfect value creation process, having zero waste generated in eight different areas: **D**efects, **O**ver-Production, **W**aiting, **N**on-Utilized Talent, **T**ransportation, **I**nventory, **M**otion, and **E**xtra-Processing or D-O-W-N-T-I-M-E.

Lean Challenges

In a lean environment, the traditional hierarchy is transformed from top-down leadership, to leadership based on questioning, coaching, and teaching, to create a new team culture guided by aspirations of leaner operations. Teams must work together to highlight and discuss obstacles and problems in a safe and supportive environment, not hide problems or recurring mistakes. Workers identify waste or expensive surplus inventory, for example, and are collectively committed to ongoing process improvements to remedy the waste or surplus. Some organizations even incent their workers by aligning lean performance savings to compensation.

Enhanced Communication Skills Required

This collaboration and culture, highlighting wasteful errors and processes, requires enhanced communication skills and leadership that guards against teams falling apart as defects, errors, lack luster management, etc. go under a microscope for all to see. This level of communication requires transparent and supportive leadership that transforms the organization in proportion to the strength of the team's communication skills and commitment to a lean culture.

Shared Open Spaces – Communicating in a Fish Bowl Can Put Some in Their Shell

The implementation of shared open space in ecosystems, where workers are free to roam and work in a variety of settings, is becoming more and more popular. The dominant support for the move to open concept and diverse communal spaces was the belief that the quality and the frequency of communication would improve in more collaborative, symbiotic working relationships. It was thought that taking down walls and bringing employees together physically would encourage interaction, cooperation, and free flowing collaborative ideas that should contribute to the quality, adoption, speed of communication, and progress.

Shared Spaces Benefits

The move to open concept was also embraced, in part, for nurturing the health and wellness of its inhabitants. Italian physician, Bernardino Ramazzini, is recognized as the founder of ergonomics in the 1700s, and his research started important thinking around how an employee's health is impacted by their work environment. Ramazzini brought awareness to reoccurring physical injuries due to repetitive movements associated with types of work in various professions. He also discussed important variations in health, depending on how long workers maintained a physical position. [2] A well-designed ecosystem addresses these concerns by providing a variety of open spaces that encourage physical movement and variety in body positioning as employees navigate the space throughout the day. This was thought to encourage not only health but health related creativity, increased focus, and rejuvenation for workspace inhabitants.

Shared Open Spaces Challenges

However, effective collaboration and sustained productivity can be elusive if the right communication skills aren't developed to work in these environments. Research done at Harvard University, by Ethan Bernstein and Stephen Turban, showed, on the basis of two field studies of corporate headquarters, that the modern open-office architecture actually decreased the number of face-to-face interactions by 70 per cent. Removing walls had the opposite effect; that is, reducing measured face-to-face interactions from 5.8 hours a day to a mere 1.7 hours on average. Some work was still getting done, and this was evidenced by a corresponding 56% increase in emails, and a 67% increase in direct messages, which became 75% longer! To make matters worse, Bernstein and Turban noted that the company's executives reported that "productivity, as defined by the metrics used in their internal performance management system, had declined after the redesign to eliminate spatial boundaries." [3]

Enhanced Communication Skills Required

The decrease in face-to-face interactions, and resulting challenges to building strong working relationships, might have been a surprise, but the decrease in productivity after the surge in email and direct messaging, shouldn't have been. Research conducted by Mahdi Roghanizad and Vanessa K. Bohns, reported in the Harvard Business Review, and published in the Journal of Experimental Social Psychology, indicated that face-to-face communication was in fact 34 times more effective than emails when collaborating with others. [4] These findings support the popular beliefs shared by many regarding the advantages of face-to-face interaction and its potential for increased communication effectiveness. However, Bernstein and Turban's work demonstrates that effective face-to-face communication demands more than just physical proximity.

Flattening Organizations Can Flatline Real Consensus

There was a time when the very telling expression, *chain of command*, meant that compliant workers executed on instructions received, without question or challenge. Sometimes instructions received morphed from the originator's intended message as it moved along the mandated chain of communicators. The all-important "why" we're moving in this direction, etc., may have also been lost along the way. That is, of course, if the "why" was ever effectively communicated to begin with. In a traditional top-down hierarchy, influence is less about inspiring someone to adopt a point of view, and more about following the chain of command and doing what you're told. For many, those days are over.

Flattening Organizations Benefits

Transforming highly hierarchical organizations, into flatter organizations with fewer levels of middle management between staff and the executive, is known as *delayering*. The predominant incentives for flattening organizations are the ability to quickly respond to new challenges; improve the speed of decision making, given fewer layers to climb up or down through; and reduce human capital expense. Flatter organizations can be more dynamic, while reducing overhead costs associated with middle management, and are believed to be inclined toward productivity. Remaining managers in flat organizations oversee larger teams, and expect subordinates to be more resourceful and autonomous. Flatter organizations shorten the chain of command, increasing communication between frontline employees and management. Front-liners, who have the relevant information and sight lines on their customers and the issues at hand, are more empowered to make more decisions. Generally, many team perspectives are shared, but often the final decision is a management stamped team decision. Hence, getting the masses to buy-in is easier for new initiatives, changes that impact the customer, profit generating ideas, etc., given that the masses were involved in the decision-making process.

Flattening Organization Challenges

There are several challenges in flatter structures outside of the logistical complications and expense in converting larger organizations. There are human relations issues that are symptomatic of converting to a flattened structure. One of these include a lower sense of employee accountability. Individuals can report to several individuals as generalists who lack clarity or significant differentiation in their roles, causing role confusion and power struggles among remaining management. Lack of incentive to perform and be promoted can be an issue, as promotions are more lateral than vertical, and flat organizations tend to produce a lot of generalists; hence, fewer specialists who garner higher compensation. Individuals who are moved into positions of leadership, do so having fewer middle management opportunities where they can learn important leadership skills in less pressurized departments before moving on.

Enhanced Communication Skills Required

In flattened organizations, the decision-making process is more of a consensus decision-making or workplace democracy. Hence, promising new ideas require the support of others to be moved forward. The leadership skill of being able to persuade and influence others outside of formal reporting lines becomes important as formal authority from direct line management is lessened or shared. Unfortunately, not all managers or team members are on equal footing when it comes to having the skills to influence other collaborators' mindsets or behaviours; hence, teams could be making decisions as we did in grade school, based on popularity contests or who best conveys power. Some teams are made of limiting homogenous gatherings, lacking diversity of thought or experience. Additionally, given that decision-making authority is closer to the front lines, it can be difficult for the executive to know for sure that all options have really been considered, and that the very best have made it to them. The ideas that get shared with the executive have been filtered, including perhaps viable ones to reorganize reporting structures that never get voiced because the masses dislike change or want to protect their jobs, etc.

In flattening organizations, individuals have to adapt to a new culture, requiring a transformation from order takers or givers borrowing authority from hierarchies, to individuals whose power comes from their ability to influence and inspire another's mindset and behaviour, leveraging their communication skills. These skills are paramount if the collective decisions made are really to represent the collective and the best options for the organization, not the popular vote, or the disproportionately powerful voices on the team who have overwhelmed the group.

The Gig Economy – Communicating with a Transient Workforce Is a Harder Gig

A gig economy is a free market system in which temporary positions are very common place, and organizations will contract with independent workers for shorter term engagements. In the digital age, more and more work is less and less dependent on being physically in the presence of your employers. With a computer and the internet, the options available stretch out globally. Examples of gig employees in the workforce include freelancers, consultants, project-based workers, independent contractors, and temporary or part-time hires.

In Canada, Randstad Canada, an HR staffing and recruiting firm, commissioned a study in 2016, and found that non-traditional workers—that is, freelancers, independent contractors, and consultants working as a non-permanent employee or on contract—already made up 20 to 30 per cent of the Canadian workforce. They go on to state that almost half of organizations are currently committed to building a variable workforce over the next five years to allow for greater flexibility and adaptability. Their projections indicate that by 2025, the majority (85%) anticipate that commitment to a flexible workforce will increase dramatically as a way to increase customer responsiveness, recession-proof their organizations, and as immunization against economic and political changes.[5] In the United States, the Bureau of Labor Statistics reported that in 2018, 55 million people in the U.S. were *gig workers*, which is more than 35% of the U.S. workforce. That number is projected to jump to 43%, by 2020.[6]

Gig Economy Benefits

Employers indicate that agility is important to ensure their ability to adjust staffing in line with changing industry demands, seasonal demands, technological advancements, and access to global talent. Additional benefits for employers include savings associated with not providing health or vacation benefits, the ability to rent smaller office spaces, and limiting their investment in training transient employees.

These more transient arrangements can appeal to the workforce as well. Seasoned employees wanting to ease out of the work force slowly, or keep one toe in for entertainment purposes, or to help fund retirement, embrace the ability to lighten the workload or dial it up should the need arise. Younger millennials, often described as frequent flyers between organizations and experiences, can find this variation in employer and experiences attractive. This transient workforce supports a better work-life balance, with many cutting their commute by working from home, having some flexibility with which hours of the day they work, and doing work that appeals to their interests.

Gig Economy Challenges

The gig economy has its challenges too. The transient workforce often loses employer paid benefits like medical, vacation time, and sick days. Employers are more reluctant to invest in training this significantly sized transient workforce; hence, the gig workforce must invest unpaid time and money into maintaining both their hard skills and softs skills to remain competitive and attractive to the market place.

Fulltime workers have a harder time progressing in their careers as temporary workers are brought into higher paying jobs that organizations don't want to staff or fund permanently. Additionally, fulltime employees can see fewer pay raises as outside talent can sometimes be found at cheaper hourly rates, and hence contribute to lower salaries.

Enhanced Communication Skills Required

Full-time employees are relied upon to demonstrate individual leadership skill and to nurture positive working relationships with the transient talent pool. This outside talent pool needs to be accepted into the circle, quickly and effectively, in order to meet project timelines and make the most of the expertise they bring to the collaboration. With the coming and going of workers in a more transient workforce, the quality of communication and collaboration can be negatively impacted on several fronts. There is little time to build quality working relationships with individuals brought in or working remotely, to contribute during a short gig. Added to this, remote workforces can be internationally dispersed partners working in contact centres, IT support, payroll offices, etc. Not only does the local workforce have to deal with physical displacement and possible time zone differences requiring workarounds, they must also learn to communicate effectively with individuals having different cultural biases and work ethics or standards. These variances require acknowledgement, additional discernment, and interpretation. Something as simple as, "I need this to be done quickly," sets differing expectations amongst differing cultures. Generally, given the gap in soft skill training, but more so with the gig workforce, fulltime employees can be burdened to close communication and collaboration gaps when working with gig employees who have the hard skills and knowledge required for a project, but lack the soft skills to influence the others to adopt them. These are the outside collaborators, sometimes described as "a tech genius but a little socially awkward."

Working conditions, like time restrictions around releases, limited physical proximity, dramatic increases in physical proximity, lack of familiarity, the unreliability of a democratic consensus, time zone adjustments, cultural anomalies, etc., bring new challenges to collaborators. This diversity is the tapestry of today's workplace. Effective communication and individual leadership skills, which filled voids in familiarity, culture, time zones, time crunches, physical displacement, or the social skills required in tight interactive groups, etc., used to be "a nice to have." In these more collaborative spaces, they have become non-negotiable.

We've seen several examples of changing workspaces; now let's have a look at changing *workfaces*.

Notes:

1   Ahlbäck K, Fahrbach C, Murarka M, and Salo O. How to Create an Agile Organization. Mckinsey.com; 2017.
2   Bernardino Ramazzini: The First Ergonomist (and what have we learned from him?). ergonomenon.com
3   Bernstein, Ethan, and Stephen Turban. "The Impact of the 'Open' Workspace on Human Collaboration." Art. 239. *Philosophical Transactions of the Royal Society B, Biological Sciences* 373, no. 1753; 2018.
4   Roghanizad M, Bohns VK. Harvard Business Review and published in the Journal of Experimental Social Psychology Volume 69, pages 223-226; 2017.
5   Randstad Canada. Workforce 2025, the future of the world of work. randstad.ca; 2016
6   Hyken S. The Gig Economy Opens The Door For Employment Opportunities. Forbes.com; 2018

Chapter Three

Navigating Increased Workforce Diversity

"What we have to do... is to find a way to celebrate our diversity and debate our differences without fracturing our communities."
– Hillary Clinton (American politician, diplomat, lawyer, former first lady of the United States, and first woman in history to be nominated for president of the United States)

"Diversity and inclusion, which are the real grounds for creativity, must remain at the center of what we do."
– Marco Bizzarri (Italian businessman; president and CEO of Gucci, 2017; 2016 International Business Leader at the Fashion Awards; received 2015 Humanitarian of the Year Award, by the United Nations Association)

Changing Workfaces

Diversity in the human workforce is just as present and important as the diversity in workplace methodologies and structures, etc. Organizations are investing in cataloguing diversity among its workforce, in part in an attempt to empower managers and others with the knowledge of how best to motivate, reward, and engage each other. The cataloguing and subsequent recommendations for behavioural guidance include areas such as personality, gender, sexual orientation, culture, generational cohorts, and variations in physical or mental ability, etc.

Sidestepping Human Diversity – Lost Creativity and Innovation

Some attempt to sidestep the diversity issue by creating homogeneous departments of nodding heads, because they're easier to influence and collaborate with. This makes the department's head or any collaborator's job easier because they don't have to master the skills to relate to or influence individuals different from themselves. But in doing so, they lose the additional potential outside their shared knowledge, experience, and reach. I've visited with companies who have told me, "We like to keep a younger vibe," where the entire team are about the same age, dress the same, talk the same, and presumably think the same, having many shared experiences and preferences. "They all just get along." Ironically, their target customers looked different from the company's workforce, were significantly older, had different values, behaved differently, and wanted for different things. This company's strategies, for recruitment, the environments/mediums they use to prospect for new sales leads, the office attire, the behaviour at reception, etc., were limited as they reflected the values, ideas, and shared experiences of their very homogeneous workforce. Anyone who has one will tell you that a diverse workforce is a gift that translates into diversity of thought, enhanced strategic ideas, varied experiences, and unique problem solving. It's a robust source for the much sought-after creativity and innovation that progressive organizations are looking for today. Hence, organizations that are keeping it young, old, white, black, male, female, etc. are missing out.

Diversity Trends Within Departments

The following are some of the trends in diversity within departments. There are opportunities, and there are challenges requiring leadership skill to bridge the *gap* in the *generation gap*, for example, and in diversity training programs themselves. Let's have a closer look at some of the diversity within departments now, and a unique way of embracing it.

Generational Cohorts – Mind the Gap

For the first time in history, we have five generations working alongside each other: traditionalists, baby boomers, Generation X, Generation Y, or millennials, and the now surfacing Generation Z (Facebook/tablet/post-millennial generation; one of these will stick eventually). Demographers, with some consistency, have grouped people into *generations*, impacted by varying political and social movements, economic hardships or opportunities, etc. that influenced the group's values and beliefs. Perceived differences in generational traits, often called "the generation gap," has been increasingly coming into focus, and is influencing meeting formats, working environments, spatial requirements, start times, dress code, supervision styles and frequency, communication format preferences, mentoring strategies, etc. Part of the current obsession for all things millennial is the sheer size of this generation. Not since the baby boomer dominance have we seen such aggressive analysis of any one generation. Millennials became the largest American workforce segment in 2016, and effective 2018, represented more than 35% of the overall workforce.[1] In Canada, millennials held the majority of the labor force, at 37% in 2015,[2] and both cohorts continue to grow. Studies vary, but some forecast that millennials will make up 75% of the workforce in the United States, by 2025, and by 2028 in Canada. It's hard not to break out into a discussion about trends, preferences, and stereotypes as they pertain to varying generations given their prevalence in the media today*. Suffice to say, millennials are in the unique position of having strength in numbers, and organizations will do well to take note of their values and preferences for engagement, and align acquisition/retention strategies, etc., as missteps will be magnified due to their sheer numbers.

*If you are interested in some of the noted differences among varying demographic cohorts or "generations," for the purpose of creating additional awareness, visit www.embracingleadershift.com for your exclusive access to our "Generation Celebration" resource that outlines birthdates, unique experiences and unique characteristics for each generation. Again, there is less information as to *why* common behaviours or trends etc. exist and no information as to why two individuals, in the same generation, will differ in the traits most often displayed. As a Leader, it's your job to embrace this diversity and work with individuals or groups on a case by case basis to best determine how to influence and inspire those you are collaborating with, who may differ considerably from yourself.

Personality Variations

Some organizations put a lot of focus on personality type profiling that indicates how different personalities perceive, judge, and come to conclusions. For example, the Myers-Briggs Type Indicator, which has been around for years, suggests 16 distinctive personality types. It highlights differences in personality attributes, such as whether you're an introvert or an extrovert, or whether you make decisions based on thinking or feeling preferences, etc. The objective is to create awareness and appreciation for the 16 personality differences, not to suggest that one is better than the other. Profiles offer insight on how to better relate and communicate with each other, while offering additional self-awareness for the assessed individual themselves. Some organizations have internally posted codes that describe each other's personalities, and with the training received, individuals are presumably more effective at communicating with each other. The intent is to be better received, meet with better collaboration, and do it in less time. Before speaking on the phone or drafting your next email, you need only glance at the individual's profile code to get insight on how to write or speak to better resonate with your audience, and get what you want. For example, are they the *teacher type?* Appeal to their sense of nurturing, and highlight your willingness to learn; now you're resonating and moving in the right direction. Some frown on cataloguing people and publishing such codes, as it's difficult to tell if people are speaking to you in a sincere manner or working your profile indicator to manipulate you.

All Persons Created Unique

The complexity increases further with the inclusion of global partners and the multitude of cultural diversity specific to different regions of the world. Where you sit at the table, whether or not you look into someone's eyes, how many hands were on your business card as you passed it, etc., all communicate something, and these variations in behaviour are as diverse as are the nations of this world. We could continue to list the diversity in the workforce and the associated training, but it would take the balance of this book! Documenting workforce diversity is not the objective of this book; communicating effectively and generating extraordinary results via enhanced leadership skills, while embracing that diversity, is.

Diversity Training Pitfalls

Diversity identification and training is a valid means to creating awareness, inclusion, communication, fairness, and equal opportunity that discourages deliberately or unintentionally alienating anyone. Our individual upbringing and culture can sometimes make us oblivious to alternatives to our understanding of the world, customs, and what we deem appropriate behaviour. Cataloguing or grouping similar people into groups based on age, ability, gender, race, etc. are important as a means of identifying and celebrating uniqueness amongst collaborators, and there are some efficiencies in being guided by profiles, given the vast diversity in a workforce, but care must be taken to guard against the belief that any one person will fit into any one mold perfectly.

In the case of personality profiling, sometimes reading lines from a script that's intended to resonate with the receiver's personality can come off as cold or even manipulative. While you might be saying all the right things that this person would normally respond well to, the receiver can't always discern the sincerity in your words, and might feel that the speaker is using *insider profiling knowledge* to manipulate the receiver into being persuaded.

When it comes to associations based on age brackets, you can't reliably make assumptions. For example, more individuals are marrying later in life or not at all. Some are starting a family later, in their forties, or not at all. Also, some are working into their later years because, financially, they have to, or because they want to, as their sustained health and passion drives them to do so etc.

Designing work benefits, or mentoring relationships, or communication formats, etc. that cater to assumptions made or stereotypes we seem to obsess about, will be less effective than identifying individual strengths, desires, motivations, etc. to influence, inspire, and generate results. Categorizing people into boxes can sometimes help us understand each other, but be careful to not make assumptions about what individuals want or need based on a lazy stereotype dependency. You need to continuously guard against well rooted assumptions that can make people feel alienated, undervalued, and demotivated. As a leader of a team, or as an individual among collaborating peers, you need to hold yourself to a higher standard of care. Be curious about who people are and what makes them tick; don't cut corners.

The Platinum Rule

Most of us are familiar with the Golden Rule that our parents or school teachers recited: *"Treat others the way you would like to be treated."* That's fine if we're talking about respect and fairness, etc., but effective leaders use a higher standard—the Platinum Rule— "Treat others the way *they* would like to be treated." How do you achieve such a standard when there are vast differences between individuals? How do you decide what approach to take that will effectively influence and inspire individuals to extraordinary results when no two people are the same? Does your behaviour have to change every time you deal with a different person? Can you have a go-to manner of conducting yourself, which both acknowledges diversity in others and taps into our similarities as an evolving species?

The challenge to successfully harness the power of a diverse workforce is a formidable one. But what if you had a process of engagement that the leader of a team or an individual leader among collaborating peers could use that sought to acknowledge and demonstrate extraordinary care in identifying preferences, rather than make assumptions based on models of catalogued individuals? Is it possible to engage everyone, leveraging the same process, and still establish enhanced communication that successfully influences, inspires, and generates extraordinary results? I'll introduce a leader's engagement process that maps out the steps on how to do this, in the next chapter.

*Visit www.embracingleadershift.com for access to exclusive bonus book materials including the "Generation Celebration" resource that outlines birthdates, unique experiences and unique characteristics for each generation.

Five Steps to Influence and Inspire Extraordinary Results™

Creating Buy-in
Casting a Vision
Establishing Trust
Building Relationships
Making a Connection

Use this *Generation Celebration* Resource to identify birthdates, unique experiences and unique characteristics for each generation.

Advanced Leadership

Generation Celebration

Notes:

1   Fry R. Millennials are the largest generation in the U.S. labor force. Pewresearch.org; 2018.
2   Mendes S. Understanding the Millennial Workforce. Restaurants Canada Blog; 2018

Chapter Four

Five Steps to Influence and Inspire Extraordinary Results™

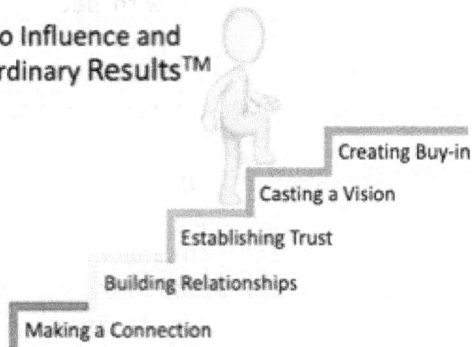

"If your actions inspire others to dream more, learn more, do more, and become more, you are a leader."
— John Quincy Adams (former president of the United States; American statesman, diplomat, lawyer, and diarist)

"Greatness comes by doing a few small and smart things each and every day. Comes from taking little steps, consistently. Comes from making a few small chips against everything in your professional and personal life that is ordinary, so that a day eventually arrives when all that's left is The Extraordinary."
— Robin S. Sharma (Canadian author of the book series, *The Monk Who Sold His Ferrari*)

Five Steps to Influence and
Inspire Extraordinary Results™

Creating Buy-in

Casting a Vision

Establishing Trust

Building Relationships

Making a Connection

It's a Process

Being an *extraordinary* leader means investing in a transparent engagement process that seeks to understand, appreciate, and leverage the uniqueness of individuals with whom you are collaborating with. The *Five Steps to Influence and Inspire Extraordinary Results*™ supports a leader's ability to do this.

Given that it's a five-step *process*, it's a repeated sequence of events. The process is always the same, but what you discover along the way will always be different depending on who you are aiming to collaborate with, as no two individuals or groups are the same.

Think of the process as a transparent fact-finding mission that seeks to put your collaborating team or peers at ease as you acknowledge their uniqueness, and leverage genuine care to uncover information that guides your next informed move. This, while presenting ideas in a way that best resonates with the manner in which individuals process information.

Each step will give you, the leader of a team, or an individual leader among collaborating peers, the opportunity to learn more about your team or peers, and provides you with the opportunity to adjust your behaviour or strategy to best inspire and influence others while supporting your mutual success. This will mean investing the time to *make a connection* with people, *building a relationship*, *establishing trust*, being able to *cast an inspiring vision* of tomorrow that people will want to follow, and creating all-important *buy-in* to gain commitment for what must be done today.

We Are More Similar Than Different

In a world obsessed with cataloguing people and focussing on our differences, it may surprise you to know just how similar we really are, and what research confirms are common strategies that humans, despite their differences, consistently respond to. The successful application of the strategies you're going to read about are not dependent on where someone was raised, the state of the economy, their age, or their gender, but rather is dependent on how humans have collectively evolved, and what individuals in successful organizations have routinely responded positively to, over decades.

In Pursuit of Excellence

I looked extensively for content that would support individuals who were striving to achieve more than just success. I wanted quality material for individuals who have an affinity for the word, *extraordinary,* when envisioning their personal or collaborative performance. I wanted a process that would allow individuals and organizations to reach such heights without having to exclude everything and everyone outside of work in order to make it happen, while others glamorize working 50, 60+ hours a week. I wanted to find proof, more than anecdotal best practices or individual success stories, that clearly demonstrated that you can achieve extraordinary results by being a powerful influencer and inspiration to those around you. I wanted evidence that you too can generate extraordinary results that far exceed the performance of the masses, by being willing to learn and implement content that the vast majorities neglect to use consistently. I wanted to find and share what the majorities fail to uncover; that is, the building blocks used by titans before them to create the successes they have built consistently over time and enhance those strategies still further, leveraging contributions from the scientific community. I wanted a process that would support a leader in eliciting *extraordinary results*, without depending on quantity engagement but rather on quality engagement while achieving *work-life balance*. I wanted to reveal a truth—that you can have both.

The Five Steps

After studying countless approaches, and sorting through corroborated claims by published acclaimed leaders in their respective fields, I created a succinct process that you as a leader can implement in five powerful steps.

The *Five Steps to Influence and Inspire Extraordinary Results*™ include:

- Making a Connection
- Building a Relationship
- Establishing Trust
- Casting a Vision
- Creating Buy-in

Don't Cut Corners

Each step informs and empowers the next. There are no skipping steps and realistically expecting extraordinary results. You cannot invite collaborators to follow you in your aspirational vision of the future without first establishing trust with them, for example. Similarly, you cannot establish trust with a collaborator who doesn't have some sort of relationship with you. You cannot inspire strong, spirited buy-in for the work that must be done today, without understanding to what aspirational vision or end the effort contributes to tomorrow. For extraordinary results, don't cut corners; start at the beginning, and commit to all five steps. Most skip back and forth, with some competence within each step, meet with some success, and then fall back again, not knowing where they went wrong. But if you've come this far in this book, you're not satisfied with the kind of success that most accept; you resonate with extraordinary—and what the masses do, has never inspired you.

We'll explore each of the *Five Steps to Influence and Inspire Extraordinary Results*[TM] in the following chapters, and then conclude with a buoyant case study that demonstrates the application of the *Five Steps to Influence and Inspire Extraordinary Results*[TM]. Let's begin with the first step: Making a Connection.

Chapter Five

Making a Connection

"In my experience, in this industry, the things that have been breakthrough[s] have all been about connecting human beings to each other, communicating with each other."
– Renee James (American technology executive, chairman and CEO of Ampere Computing, and former president of Intel)

"I don't know what life was like 1,000 years ago, but I imagine there was the same struggle: people trying to connect with each other."
– Spike Jonze (American filmmaker; Academy Award, Golden Globe, and Writers Guild of America Award winner)

Five Steps to Influence and
Inspire Extraordinary Results™

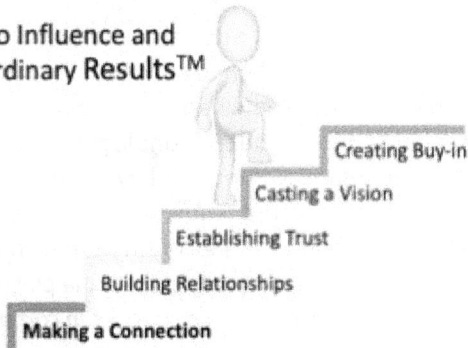

Creating Buy-in

Casting a Vision

Establishing Trust

Building Relationships

Making a Connection

The Importance of Connecting

You may have witnessed what two different individuals can accomplish with the same group. One person can give a set of instructions or demands, and everyone nods their heads in unison but fail to take any significant action, or do just enough to "stay under the radar." Another person, of equal or even lesser authority, can ask for the same thing, and the whole team starts buzzing with activity and producing results above and beyond what is contractually required of them. Why the difference in outcome? The difference in the ability to influence the audience, of one or many, comes down to not who has more authority but instead, who has a stronger connection with the target audience. Sometimes you can get an employee's attention more readily because you have a bigger title, but that doesn't always make a difference when it comes to actual output once your back is turned. Sure, you can watch a parade of flying paper and activity, but that doesn't mean that anything of substance is getting done.

Why are you compelled to vote for one politician over another when by the end of their campaigns, they all start to sound alike, regardless of the political party they represent? It's likely you've made a connection with one of the candidates or the party they represent, despite the similarities in their campaigns or the messages they share. You probably connected with one more than the other, perhaps as a result of watching them on TV portraying *physiology,* like the open hand gestures they've been coached to use that signals that they're trustworthy. Maybe you attended a town hall where you witnessed the candidate actively *listen* to residents vent about community issues, and then were surprised when the candidate accurately summarized the resident's four-minute monologue in a 20-second summary. Maybe you were really impressed by the tireless *effort* this candidate put in across their riding, knowing full-well they spent many hours away from the family that they often shared and talked about. It might be that this candidate showed up at all the places you visit on a regular basis, and as it turns out, you have a lot *in common* with them, maybe even attending the same local high school! Lastly, you know that the candidate is a politician, and politicians are known for making lots of promises, but there is something about this candidate's ability to open up and speak from the heart, while not being afraid to speak to *emotionally* charged topics that really inspired you. All of the traits of purposeful physiology, listening, finding common ground, giving genuine effort, and possessing emotional intelligence are required when building a strong connection to support a leader's ability to influence, inspire, and generate extraordinary results. Let's look at a few ways you can strengthen your ability to successfully connect so as to better your chances of effective communication and, ultimately, generate extraordinary results.

Physiology – It's Beyond Words

In a collaborative environment, everyone can physically or virtually see *you!* The person(s) you are aiming to persuade or influence is consciously, or unconsciously, noticing what your posture, voice tonality, movements, etc. are intentionally or unintentionally communicating.

One of the easiest things to do when successfully *connecting* is becoming aware of your physiology. According to Dr. Albert Mehrabian's 7-38-55 Rule of Personal Communication, words only make up 7% of any message, but voice tonality and body language contribute 38% and 55% respectively to the intended emotional meaning of a message.[1] You must master what you are personally conveying, and be able to identify in others, demonstrated or curiously absent physiology that sends powerful signals about where you are coming from, your emotions, the real emotional meaning behind your words, and whose interests you are serving. These are the subtle details that many will miss; for example, fluctuations in one's eye movements, changes in posture, voice inflection, changes in the colour of one's face, or the ability to read the palpable energy between the speaker and their audience, etc.

This is why I prefer to meet coaching clients face-to-face, as telephone conversations are overly dependent on deciphering meaning via voice tonality and word selection alone. When someone isn't visible, it's impossible to pick up on the change in physical signals like posture, leaning, or a tempered smile that communicates emotions like hesitation or enthusiasm about this month's development plan, for example. Video conferencing helps a lot, but nothing beats face-to-face, where what you feel, smell, and the more you see, adds greater meaning to the message being delivered.

Test It

See what a difference physiology, and by extension, voice tonality, makes when accompanied by the same set of words. Here's an example I like to perform in workshops, because it really brings out an "aha" reaction from the crowd. Try it by yourself or with a feedback-sharing friend. Say the exact same words but use different physiology and voice tonality. What's so interesting is that I could spend a page telling you what I do physically or what I do with my voice to demonstrate two very different meanings using the same words, but the instruction is not necessary. All I have to do is give you guidance on how you feel as you say the statement two different ways. Your physiology and voice tonality will communicate a message about your beliefs or emotions automatically. Don't believe it's that simple? It is. Perform the following sentence twice. I say "perform" because how you communicate is more than just your mouth saying words; your voice tonality and body will be communicating as well. You should stand up so that more movements are available to you. What you do may even surprise yourself. Take out your smartphone to record yourself, or get a friend to describe in vivid detail what they saw and felt. During the first round, say it as a well-intending, supportive supervisor, who provides generous access to employees requiring assistance. During the second round, say it as the supervisor who dislikes being unexpectedly approached, and feels that employees should find answers on their own. Here is the statement:

"Mike, so glad you came to me with this problem you are having, and at this late hour. Come on in, come on in."

I usually get two very different reactions from the audience. For the first round, feedback includes: the supervisor was "cheerful" and "helpful." The second round gets comments like "bone-chilling," "dripping with sarcasm," and "unsupportive." The same exact words were spoken, yet what was communicated was entirely different.

There's no such thing as *not* communicating emotions, unless you've been practicing your neutral gaze at the poker table. You can leave people not knowing what you really mean, but that will just make them guess what you mean—and sometimes guess very wrong. This, of course, is the exact opposite of what we're aiming to achieve. We are striving for clear, purposeful, and intentional communication to support collaboration and extraordinary results.

Thankfully, being aware of your physiology is like developing any new skill, and is just the sustainment of a new good habit that comes with learning, implementation, and consistent application. As you become more aware of your physiology, and are committed to more consistently ensuring that your physiology matches your intended emotional meaning, it will eventually become second nature, and your effectiveness, as it relates to communication, will improve. Eventually, haphazard unintended physiological habits, or *behavioural tics,* will be replaced by intentional purposeful habits that clearly communicate your intended meaning.

Listening – Listening at a Whole New Level

As the leader of a department, or as a leader among collaborating peers, your ability to connect and ultimately influence others depends on your ability to listen to them.

Adults were asked, in a study, to describe content after listening in for 10 minutes. Moments later, only 50% of adults could describe the content, and 48 hours later, only 25% could.[2] Were these individuals listening or merely hearing? Listening is not a passive activity, and it involves more than just passively hearing someone. Listening is an active skill, requiring effort. Underdeveloped listening skills challenge our individual and collaborative effectiveness regularly. Great leaders and collaborators take their listening to a whole new level.

Listening plays an important role in gathering pertinent details, honoring someone, and reducing misunderstandings. Listening helps you determine what motivates different individuals or cohorts, inspires commitment to objectives, helps you find solutions that better resonate with your target audience, and is mandatory when making a connection with someone.

Would it surprise you to learn that to a great extent, effective leadership means effective listening? In research conducted by R. Kramer, listening accounted for 40% of the variance in leadership assessment.[3] That is, as a leader of a team or as an individual leader among collaborating peers, your employees or group can see you doing many things right, but effective listening will contribute to 40% of their assessment of your leadership skills. This is at odds with images for leadership in the media, which often portray a leader speaking to a group or taking some action that others follow; rarely is the leader presented as the one unceremoniously doing the listening.

Do you want to empower yourself with the ability to influence others, as the leader of a team or as a leader among your collaborating peers? Do you want to improve your leadership assessment scores? Try taking your listening skills to a new level. There are three levels of listening that a leader must master in order to connect and better position themselves to influence, inspire, and generate extraordinary results.

Level One: *It's All About Me, Me, Me*

A level one listener will hear words spoken while being bombarded by their inner voice, constantly interrupting with self-reflection, and inserting themselves into the meaning that they assume the speaker is communicating. For example, a listener's inner voice might contribute, "I wonder what I would do in that situation?" This listener can hardly wait for their turn to speak, and often jumps to start telling their version or story when the speaker merely takes a breath. This listener won't go back to what the speaker was saying, because they didn't even notice a gap in the incomplete story, as they weren't really listening in the first place. A level one listener is more mentally focussed on deciding what to say next than understanding what the speaker is saying. This level one listener is deciphering meaning based on any words they hear, and what those words mean to them, based on their personal experience and biases. The speaker might say that "she's sick," which could mean that she needs a doctor, but it could also mean that she's hip or praise worthy. Many words have multiple meanings in the English language, and a level one listener will just assume that the speaker has adopted the same meaning they use.

A colleague might ask for *an excellence customer experience*, but if you ask an IT person, or compliance and regulations person, or a marketing person what would comprise *an excellent customer experience*, each person will describe the experience differently. The IT person might want speed in the transaction, with zero glitches, and a speedy checkout. The compliance and regulations person might prefer that the customer be deliberately slowed down to review all disclosures up front, and require evidence that the customer read and understood the risks in doing business together, before moving forward. A marketing person might prefer emotionally charged images at the top of the webpage and throughout, that communicated the feeling a customer is expected to have once they start doing business with the group. A level one listener will just decide for themselves what the speaker meant. A level one listener has taken away *an understanding*, but it may not be *the understanding* that the speaker intended. Level one conversations are more prone to misunderstandings, and any recommended solutions often insufficiently address the speaker's concerns. The "conversation," and the poorly informed proposed solution, can leave the speaker feeling unheard, disrespected, or unappreciated.

Level Two: *I Hear the Words You Speak*

A level two listener sets aside their inner voice and chatter. This listener does not interrupt; they listen intently to all words spoken, nod, and may even summarize the speaker's words to further demonstrate that they heard the speaker. Most individuals operating at this level would be described as a *good listener*. When a speaker is just looking for a shoulder to cry on, this level of listening will usually suffice.

At this level, while the listener "heard" what the speaker said accurately, they are again deciphering meaning based on any words they hear, and the biased meaning that the listener assigns to them. For example, a dad might be talking to his son, who has asked for access to knowledge because he has every intention of doing well at school this year. The next day, Dad shows up with a set of encyclopedias. The disappointed speaker (the son) asks, "What am I to do with those? I wanted a powerful computer and high-speed internet." Dad is a level two listener, and in his defense, he says, "But you said you wanted access to knowledge." And his son (the speaker) says, "Yes, I said those words, but that's not what I meant." Unfortunately, Dad, the level two listener, hasn't done the extra work to confirm the speaker's meaning. In a solution manufacturing environment, level two listening is also prone to misunderstanding and weaker solutions based on assumptions made by the listener, despite the speaker feeling heard initially.

Level Three: Listening Like a Leader – *Please Help Me Understand*

A level three listener is curiously aware of their inner voice and chatter, listens without interrupting, and repeats content back, to demonstrate that they were listening...

AND does the following:

A level three listener uses open-ended questions to gather additional perspective and check for understanding. They will ask questions like, "What does an excellent customer experience look like to you?" Or they will say, "Tell me more about that," etc.

A level three listener is careful not to use the word, *why*, in their line of questioning, as it can sometimes invite defensiveness. Instead, level three listeners will ask questions like, "What is it about XYZ that makes you feel unappreciated?" This is far better received than, "Why are you feeling unappreciated?"

A level three listener is aware of Dr. Albert Mehrabian's 7-38-55 Rule of Personal Communication, that is, words only communicate 7% of the emotional meaning of any message, and that voice tonality and body language contribute 38% and 55% respectively to the intended emotional meaning of a message.[4] They are master observers of expression and subtle details that others miss, like the speaker's feet that are now pointed at the door as, subconsciously, they are disclosing that they don't want to be in this conversation any longer. What the speaker wants is to be on the other side of that door, and away from the listener. A level three listener can pick this up without the speaker being consciously aware that they disclosed it.

A level three listener gently tunes in to that inner voice. As a leader, you are continuously striving to grow. Part of the process of building emotional intelligence, specifically self-awareness, includes a healthy amount of self-reflection to build your personal awareness of how your own biases are influencing your interpretation of the communication and your decision making. As a continuously evolving leader, it's productive to be curious about how you're feeling, and why, as you listen. When a peer says, "I need to get home; something has come up," a leader might catch their inner voice saying, "Well, your personal life must be more important than your career." The leader might then ask themselves, "Where did that come from? What is it about my personal experience that made me think that way? Why can't work and home both merit attention?"

Listening at a leadership level 3 will give you better insight, and will empower you to more effectively influence and make recommendations that better align with what your colleagues, and your team, are communicating they want. In addition to increased effectiveness, your effort will distinguish you among your peers, while enhancing your leadership assessment scores. By using all three levels of listening, you can make a speaker feel heard, and learn a lot about their needs, what motivates them, who they are, and perhaps, a little more about who you are.

Investing Discretionary Effort – How to Get an 'A' for Effort

Another crucial requirement for making a connection with an audience, of one or many, is that audience's ability to identify the investment of discretionary effort. When you give of yourself, you've invested limited quantities of your time and energy. Both of these are valuable resources that everyone can personally relate to; hence, audiences appreciate when you share them in order to make them feel special, welcomed, or included. That effort is appreciated even more when the effort made was above and beyond what was required of you.

How Are Things Outside Work?

Checking in with your team or collaborating partners goes a long way toward forming strong connections. Simple gestures like asking, "How are you?" may seem unimportant outside the scope of work, or may even seem inappropriate in meetings. I struggled with this for years. I never wanted people to think that I overstepped our level of rapport, or that I was meddling somehow in someone's personal life. I usually waited until that person shared something personal, and that would be my green light to wade in gently and genuinely. As a leader, sometimes it's easier not to ask things you can't *unhear*. It may be the easier way, but that doesn't mean it's the right way, and it certainly won't help your ability to connect with your team or collaborating peers. Research shows the positive side of taking interest in the lives of others outside of work. Karyn Twaronite writes, in the Harvard Business Review, about a study that looks at humans' innate need to belong, and found that people are more productive, motivated, and 3.5 times more likely to contribute to their full potential when they feel like they belong. The research further showcases the power of checking in with colleagues. It was reported that "39% of respondents feel the greatest sense of belonging when their colleagues check in with them, personally or professionally. This was true across genders and age groups, with checking in being the most popular tactic for establishing a sense of belonging across all generations. By reaching out and acknowledging their employees on a personal level, companies and leaders can significantly enhance the employee experience by making their people feel valued and connected." [5] Checking in on someone with something as simple as asking, "How are you?" acknowledges first and foremost who we are; that is, interacting individual human beings who have a life outside work, who come together to achieve great things.

If you're going to ask, "How are you?" you had better be asking genuinely. It can be irritating and condescending to be asked by someone, "How are you?" only to have them jump into the real purpose of their visit, and never wait to hear the response to the question. I still hear this in retail spaces, where the clerk doesn't even make eye contact, or wait for the answer, before asking if you found everything you were looking for. If this is your current default setting, you'd be better received or supported by not asking the question. But you'd be missing a fascinatingly simple way to connect and engage with your team or collaborating peers. It is a commitment of your time, and not an absolute requirement of your job. It's the investment of energy and effort you made outside of job requirements that makes it appreciated.

You might be afraid of getting stuck in a lengthy conversation with *a talker* who wants to tell you about their lactose intolerant cat. If someone is expressing something of great concern to them, let them speak, because if it's the first thing out of their mouth, it's also the first thing on their mind. The personal issue and possible distraction is a hurdle you'll have to clear anyway, or else you'll have that obstacle constantly challenging this person's attention and focus. Whatever the individual discusses may be of little relevance or of little importance to you, but here's what's important: it matters to them. Investing some time to hear them out shows that you are interested in them and their universe. You need not fix anything or offer advice on how to resolve the issue—just make the effort to ask, and be a good listener. Certainly, if you have knowledge of in-house or external resources they can use, you can ask if they would appreciate you facilitating access to those resources. It should go without saying; any serious physical or mental crisis that someone communicates should be immediately referred to someone who is qualified to assess the situation and determine the appropriate plan of action. That may or may not be you.

Here are a couple of tips I share in our Connecting for Influence Workshop™, which work to acknowledge the individual's non-crisis share and transition back to work related items, when the conversation has gone into unproductive territory. These responses work, but you must absolutely say them with a genuine heart.

If the update is a positive one, say something along the lines of: "I'm glad to hear that; I wish you much continued success. I wanted to talk about building success in other areas where you shine. Do you have a few minutes for me now?"

If it's a negative update, say something along the lines of: "I'm sorry to hear that; I hope things work out for the best in the end. I wanted to talk about a project where I think you can add great value. Do you feel okay to spend some time now, discussing a few ideas? Would you appreciate the distraction?"

In most cases, your employee or collaborating colleague just wants to be heard and have parts of their personal life, outside work, acknowledged. Making the extra effort contributes to the perception that you are more approachable and relatable, even if you don't share anything about yourself. This rapport goes a long way to encouraging engagement. Gallop's "State of the American Manager" research studies 2.5 million manager-led teams in 195 countries, and features analysis that measures the engagement of 27 million employees. Gallup reported that employees who *strongly agreed* that 'they could talk to their manager about non-work-related issues" were 47% more engaged than the group who *strongly disagreed.* [6] If you aren't doing this already, it's a quick fix once you get your head around the positive impact that it makes towards making a connection.

Many people hear, "How are you?" but are unsure if the other person is really interested, and they offer the flat, unrevealing, "I'm good," because they have a popular bias or don't believe that the asker wants to hear much else. Here are a few other options you can use in place of the generic, "How are you?" These will overcome that popular bias, and help reflect that you are asking with genuine interest.

Questions you could ask to support a connection with your team or collaborating colleague:

- *How is life outside work?*
- *What is one thing you could change at work that could improve things at home?*
- *Are you celebrating the XYZ holiday? What do you usually do on that day?*
- *What do you like to do with your free time? Do you have any hobbies?*
- *How are your children doing? What activities are they interested in (or something related to the age of the child, like starting school, graduation, or selecting a university, etc.)?*

Everyone understands the value of time. It's the currency we spend, knowing we can never generate more of it. That said, this is why spending it on or with someone is most often universally appreciated. Similarly, everyone appreciates invested discretionary effort that wasn't *required*, because it draws on limited amounts of energy available to us, which we shared or invested in others.

Effort Expressed in Action Speaks Louder Than Words

I used to enjoy the challenge of starting at a new branch when I worked for one of the larger financial institutions in Canada, each one larger than the last, and having greater challenges with respect to group dynamics and market opportunities. My go-to-plan of integration was to invest in the staff, and the staff helped invest in our customers, and the customers helped invest in our financial success. Our sequential jumps in satisfaction indexes for employee engagement, customer experience, and financial results demonstrated the validity of this continuum's reliability. Shareholder value was always of great importance, but focussing on employees and our customers, which ultimately generated shareholder return, was the best way I knew how to create value for our investors and still sleep soundly at night. I used to tell my staff how much they were valued, how qualified they were to deliver on our customer's financial needs, and how important they were to our success... because they were all these things, but some of them didn't hear it enough or believe it. You can talk yourself into exhaustion and, in the end, actions prove who you are; words only express who you envision yourself to be....

Toronto winters can be months of cold, gray days that seem to never end. Employees who are dressed in business attire rarely invest the time to suit up in winter gear for a lunch hour stroll and a breath of fresh air. At best, our downtowners make their way through vast unground paths that put many street level storefronts to shame. But even these busy underground paths are no match to the fresher outside air and ice-covered sidewalk patios waiting to be opened in the spring. My teams, in our locations, were sequestered to a lounge during their winter lunch hours. In older buildings, that usually meant somewhere in the back or basement of the building, which was secure but devoid of sunlight as there were no windows. I took it upon myself, at each location, to invest some effort and make the most of the space to ensure the team was taking their breaks, felt rested, and enjoyed a mental break. Most importantly, I wanted them to know how appreciated and important they were to me, how important they were to our mutual success and to make a connection.

I would plan and shop for weeks. Then, on the weekend, I would sneak into the bank and work for most of the weekend, making over the staff lounge. Gone were the tired, broken furniture pieces, and the chipped mismatched dishes and glasses. The coffee maker and microwave oven, which looked and smelled like a Petri dish, were retired to make room for a new microwave oven and coffee maker that accompanied new bright white dishes, glassware, and cutlery. The cupboards and fridge were washed. The walls got two coats of a summer yellow paint, which were lit by newly installed accent lighting that showcased an entire wall filled with cartoon caricatures of each of my team members. I hired a student artist to draw them for me, and I framed them with great excitement in anticipation of their responses. I only had to tell a little white lie to get them to pose for me so that I could sneak photos off to the artist. The team's reaction on Monday morning was a consistent mouth dropping one. They always asked, "Why did you do this?" It was the perfect opportunity to communicate words that aligned with the effort: "Because you matter to me; you're important, and I want you to feel valued." The effort was always rewarded with a great connection that genuinely conveyed care. Nothing enduring, including a connection, is created in just one event; you need to be consistent—but these staff lounge makeovers were always a great start. Today, I remind clients that anyone can build amazing connections via invested energy. You just need commitment, consistency, a little creativity, and visibility to make it work.

I Saw That

You can do great things and not tell anyone about them. Acts of kindness are of course very rewarding personally, and almost everyone enjoys brightening someone's life with something pleasantly unexpected, but anonymity doesn't help make a connection. When you're cultivating a connection as a building block for great successes that you'll share with your team, these gestures should be visible, strategic, and purposefully dispersed across the team you lead or collaborate with. This makes your effort even more appreciated, as you've taken the time to ensure that no one gets left out, and you've done the homework to determine what would be best appreciated by a diverse team. I used to make the mistake of primarily celebrating successes that were KPIs (key performance indicators), along with the odd "caught you doing something awesome" certificates that many organizations now use. Generally, KPIs were centered on customer meetings and sales, etc. During morning huddles, I noticed the service department staff disengage a little, and talking about their referral activities to sales officers didn't always create a wow factor. This was especially true for the hard-working service team members in the back office, who were setting up products in the system, and cranking out all the documentation and files for customers to sign, which were done in-house at the time.

I took it upon myself to pull an entire busy months' worth of product set-up reports, and counted every single visa, loan, and mortgage set up by individual officer ID. This took some time and effort, but I can still see the look of gratitude as I acknowledged the volumes of work done by our support staff, who often went unnoticed. They felt appreciated and were thankful for the invested discretionary effort it took to uncover the data. They reminded me of that for months to come. It was also an eye opener for the balance of the service and sales teams. We love to win and hit the numbers that get recognized as success metrics, but it's important to recognize everyone who contributes to that success in less visible ways, to ensure that they know they are appreciated. The same is true for your efforts. As a leader, you are your own public relations representative; make sure those around you know who you are, and what you're made of—don't keep it a secret. Kind or supportive anonymous gestures are fine if you're playing secret Santa or are looking for points in the afterlife, but they won't help you make a connection with others in this one.

Common Ground – Unity, not Uniformity

Connecting is all about others, and finding common ground is one of the most important aspects of connecting, be it an audience of one or of many. Finding common ground is an important first step when building unity, not uniformity, amidst genuine diversity. A homogeneous team, lacking in diversity, will have members with similar backgrounds, experiences, values, and thoughts, will generate a limited number of ideas toward a solution. Alternatively, a diverse team's strength is the variation in life experiences, career experiences, beliefs, values, and varied thoughts that serve as references for a greater variety of ideas when tackling the same problem. Common ground is what brings us together in diversity, not what makes us the same, and is an important beginning to build on for creating larger agreements of mutually satisfying next steps. Common ground easily slips from view in conflict situations. Team positions can become polarized and exaggerated as each person aims to persuade, manipulate, or undermine another, and come out as the self-proclaimed victor. The mindset of *agree to nothing, and don't commit our resources to anything*, in a battle of manipulation, can be comical and sad at the same time—as if merely acknowledging the other side's perspective, on anything, would somehow give them additional leverage and lessen ours. Research suggests that effective negotiators point out areas of agreement three times more often than ineffective negotiators.[7]   When conversations seem to have hit an impasse, effective negotiators will go back to shared perspectives to reenergize a negotiation, over and over again.

Truth be told, we all have an agenda as part of a team or an organization. That is, we all have individual responsibilities, and make unique, important individual contributions, despite shared organizational goals and objectives. We can sometimes lose sight of these shared goals and objectives, as we get wrapped up in our own agenda, and start trying to control others as opposed to collaborating with them.

Where to Start When Building Common Ground

Your mission, should you choose to accept it, is understanding. Even if you end up disagreeing, listening for, probing for, and demonstrating your willingness to understand someone's perspective, signals your positive intentions, and is an effective negotiation strategy. The other party might even thank you for hearing them out, and you certainly should thank them for allowing you the opportunity to express your point of view. Another tactic you might consider is giving the other party the floor first. This is also an effective negotiation strategy for a number of reasons. If you hear your colleagues out, you'll understand how they might have come to certain conclusions. *You may not have reached the same conclusions*, but nonetheless, *you can understand* where their hesitancy came from, and just as important, understand what you'll need to do or offer to mitigate that hesitancy. Your prepared speech might be an arsenal of accurate facts that are completely off the mark in terms of satisfying the other side's concerns. Listen first, understand what you need to address, and leave the balance of your distracting monologue on standby. Remember to focus on larger, shared objectives to bring you to common ground. Often, it's not what you're aiming to achieve that is a point of disagreement but rather how each party aims to achieve it.

Common Ground Across Europe

People who overlook areas of common ground, miss opportunities to acknowledge, learn, and build upon what they already have in common; hence, they start at ground zero. As you understand someone's point of view, you can begin to appreciate and leverage this understanding to create viable solutions for a mutually satisfying way forward. Anne Mulrine Grob wrote, *In Search of a Common Ground: How Debate Is Bringing Europeans Together."* She describes the "Europe Talks" event that was the mastermind of editors at the German newspaper, *Die Zeit*. The event was hosted on the eve of parliamentary elections and brought together debating candidates who travelled over 500 miles, and dozens who travelled over 1000 miles, from all over Europe, to attend. While the initial event was forecasted to generate one or two hundred applicants via an online application process, over twelve thousand Europeans registered for an opportunity to debate their perspectives on the future of Europe. Some of the surveying questions to identify varying view points from Europeans having different political persuasions included:

- "Should the European Union (EU) increase taxes to help save the environment?"
- "Are there too many migrants in Europe?"
- "Should richer European countries support poorer ones?"
- "Should Europe have closer ties with Russia?"

Participants were paired up and started conversations in designated locations that spilled out into cafes and bars, etc. They each got to learn about each other as people, despite their political persuasions. When one engineer expressed a strong differing opinion on same-sex living arrangements, her debating partner, a hardened police officer, was persuaded to "soften (his) strong opinion on it." Meeting the engineer in a relaxed setting, and getting to know a bit about her while making a connection and finding some common ground, inspired him to think differently. When prompted, the police officer indicated that his willingness to think more broadly was driven by his unwillingness to hurt his new debating partner. In another example, in response to the question, "Would you give up your national passport for a European one?" a German said that he would give up his German identity in favor of a European citizenship. The debate partner, from Denmark, preferred to hold on to his Danish passport. But after meeting each other, making a connection, and discovering some common ground, the Danish citizen volunteered, while pointing to the Danish royal crown crest, "We could put Euro stars here, and maybe Denmark in smaller letters...." [8] Despite differing political persuasions and polarized initial opinions about giving up their national passports, finding common ground in a relaxed environment served as a catalyst for finding creative collaborative solutions, which included redesigning the Danish passport to demonstrate the EU alliance *and* Danish roots.

If you overlook areas of common ground, you'll miss opportunities to acknowledge, learn, and build upon what you already have in common. As we understand someone's point of view, we can begin to appreciate and leverage this new found understanding to create viable, creative, and mutually satisfying collaborative solutions. In this European example, it's not unusual that debating partners started to soften their opposing views after finding common ground. Finding common ground encouraged debating partners to have positive feelings or positive emotional reactions toward their debate partners, and tapping into emotions is a game changer.

Emotional Connections Are Powerful Ones

When making a connection with an audience of one or many, it involves understanding and leveraging our emotions and the emotions of others. Do you recall the last time you donated to a cause? Did you donate primarily because of the number of afflicted individuals, the number of government dollars currently directed toward this ailment, or the worsening prevalence throughout the population? Or were you touched by the images of suffering children, who looked into your eyes and, without saying a word, stirred your emotions, touched your heart, and compelled you to donate? The last time a motivational speaker influenced you to take action and make some changes in your life, did they share a spreadsheet that spoke to the successes of previous audience members and how they fared after pursuing a recommended path? Did the shared implementation metrics, broken down by gender or occupation, resonate with you and hence inspire you to action? Or, after listening to the speaker's personal story and empathizing with their challenges, determination, etc., you were moved both emotionally and to action, having connected with a fellow human being?

How many times have you heard that the best salespeople don't sell products; they cater to and sell emotional responses. In the famous presentation for "sell me that pen," the pen has ink in it, as do others, and was wrapped in metal, as are others, but the successful salesperson doesn't focus on the functionality of the pen that it shares with all other pens—the salesperson focusses on the emotional attachment of its potential user. That is, the prestige and pride of ownership for an accomplished individual who would write with a pen of such fine calibre. The pen isn't just a writing tool; it's an icon that speaks to the character of its user. The potential owner looks down at it and has an emotional connection to it, as that pen elicits strong feelings from the prospect, who is then compelled to buy it. Tapping into emotion creates a stronger connection to a desired end state, be it donating, changing your life, or making a purchase.

There is currently much discussion around the importance of emotional intelligence for any successful leader, and many organizations reflect this sensitivity to emotional awareness in evolving hiring processes. In some cases, you won't even get an interview until you've submitted to an emotional intelligence test that offers insight into your *soft skills* and ability to interact with people. Let's have a closer look at what emotional intelligence is, and how being attuned to your emotions, and those of others, can help you make a connection to better influence, inspire, and generate extraordinary results.

Emotional Intelligence – Managing Emotions to Make Connections

Emotional intelligence (EI), emotional leadership (EL), emotional quotient (EQ), and emotional intelligence quotient (EIQ), is an individual's ability to identify their own emotions and the emotions of others. It's the ability to discern between different feelings and label them appropriately, use emotional information to guide thinking and behaviour, and manage and/or adjust emotions to adapt to environments or achieve one's goals. [9]

There are several emotional intelligence (EI) models that are centered on emotional ability and emotional traits, or a mix of the two. Daniel Goleman was the American psychologist who first popularized emotional intelligence, and defined EI as the array of skills and characteristics that drive leadership performance. Goleman's model was of the mixed variety, and included five key elements:

- Self-awareness
- Self-regulation
- Motivation
- Empathy
- Social skills

Self-Awareness

Self-awareness speaks to a leader's ability to identify their own feelings, how those feelings influence their personal performance, and how they influence others around them. It also includes a deliberate process of identifying and developing strategies to leverage or accommodate leadership strengths and weaknesses. Finally, self-awareness includes examining personal contributions, and leading with humility.

How to Develop Self-Awareness

I encourage clients to keep a private journal of thoughts. You can do this on your locked smart device, in a notebook application. Documenting one's thoughts rapid fire, without thinking about them initially, will help you deal with all your emotions on a topic. It will feel good to acknowledge them, even if you never speak them. You might be surprised to have conflicting emotions, like being angry in having to deal with XYZ, but being happy that Suzy had the courage to bring her observation forward, etc.

Reflecting on your documented thoughts will help you plan how to navigate the situation, having cultivated insights into your own biases or personal pain points that could cloud your judgement. Jack Canfield, who I had the pleasure of meeting earlier this year, is a *New York Times* best-selling author, co-creator of the *Chicken Soup for the Soul* series, and the author of *The Success Principles*. In *The Success Principles*, Jack states that all outcomes equal an initial event, plus your subsequent response, and he stresses that you can't always control the event, but you can control your response; hence, the outcome. That said, at the first sign of anger or strong emotion, slow down long enough to figure out why you're feeling the way you do, and acknowledge just how normal the reaction might be. Ensure that your performance or response to any event is guided by self-aware, productive contributions to thinking or problem solving, and absent of negative, emotionally charged contributions, to ensure that you get the outcome you want.

Self-Regulation

Self-regulation speaks to a leader's ability to stay in control. In the face of chaos, stay calm and set an example for others, while inspiring confidence in the plan, the vision, and in you as a leader.

How to Develop Self-Regulation:

Give thought to and document your personal values that guide your life and who you want to be. Doing this work upfront allows you to filter any content thrown at you, and respond in accordance to your values, not the common reaction to what was thrown at you. Think about your response; if it doesn't meet your values, you need to adjust your behaviour. This makes most decisions far easier to make. Other processes like weighing the pros and cons, is a much lengthier process that lacks consistency.

Hold yourself accountable by admitting to your mistakes and committing to righting a wrong where you can. While admitting to a temporary failure or oversight might seem counterintuitive to fostering a leadership profile, most people will respect you for owning your mishap, and be inspired by your example to strive for your goals despite falling and having to dust yourself off occasionally. You are reducing paralyzing fear of failure in the team, and signalling that progress outweighs perfection at the price of progress. A marathon runner doesn't throw in the towel when they fall; they get up, adjust, repair or tape what they can, and keep going.

Practice the discipline of allowing others to speak first. Especially in a tense situation, let them run out of gas. This will contribute to calming them down, as they feel you are hearing them out, and they'll likely feel better, at least initially, for having voiced their opinion. This gives you a chance to assess your emotions and prevent yourself from saying or doing something outside your preferred character. You can also make the greatest contribution and impact when you fully understand someone else's feelings instead of assuming what they are.

Consider taking notes. This suggests that you're listening and taking the conversation seriously. It also slows the conversation down, and gives you the time to get your emotions in check. If you still haven't calmed down sufficiently to address the issue in a manner that's in keeping with your values, walk away after genuinely thanking the individual for the information. Advise them that you will need some time to think about the important information shared. Don't procrastinate; decide on next steps, and keep your word to follow up with a sense of urgency. Your calm in the face of chaos will encourage other's confidence in you, your vison, and the plan you put forth.

Motivation

Motivation speaks to a leader's defined and targeted goals/ambitions. Disciplined leaders are self-driven to achieve their goals, and are sensitive to the quality of outcomes that are associated with their performance.

How to Develop Motivation:

Take stock of your passions and what your purpose is. What are your strengths? Does this role allow you to play to your strengths, and to shine? Every company, and everyone, can speak to *what* they do and *how* they do things, but it is far rarer to hear a company or a leader share *why* they do what they do. For example, the value they contribute to society, to education, to the environment, etc. Figure out your why, and keep your eye on the big picture to hold your motivation.

Stay optimistic. Optimism makes us focus on the silver lining in all situations and what's going well. This builds positive reinforcement, encouragement, and momentum for more good things to come. Leaders motivated by the expectation of good things to come, tend to see more of them. Think about when you bought your last car. You bought the model that you were attracted to, and it seemed especially right and unique to your preferences. Two days later, suddenly it seems like every tenth car looks like yours. No, your neighbors didn't all buy new cars in the last two days; they were always there, but you weren't looking for them. The cars, much like the positive in any situation, were always there and went undetected because you weren't looking for them. Your subconscious mind protects you from the millions of data you are perceiving at any one time, by narrowing your focus to what has traditionally been useful information. Your subconscious is protecting you from becoming overwhelmed and paralyzed with indecision. Knowing how your subconscious mind is wired, you can use your conscious mind to purposefully target information that serves your intention to be optimistic. Repeatedly affirming to your subconscious that "there is a creative way out of this, and I will find it!" is enough to open the door. Eventually, your subconscious will say, "Oh, I guess you want to see more options now, and give up some of these negative belief paradigms that convinced you to keep the status quo because it's safer." Now, the brilliance that is your subconscious will search for new creative solutions, even in your sleep, because your conscious mind demanded it. Your optimism will bring creative solutions that others, who don't share your motivation, can't see.

Empathy

Empathy speaks to the old adage of walking in someone else's shoes, living their life, or seeing the world through someone else's eyes and, therefore, having the ability to experience another's feelings. Empathy is not sympathy, which is caring about and understanding the suffering of others. The difference is subtle but important, as it can impact appropriate behaviour or responses. For example, let's say that a parent has the experience of suffering the loss of a child, and someone who has never had a child says, "I know what you're going through." Never having had a child, this well-intending person can care about and understand the parent's suffering but cannot experience the same feelings that the definition of empathy requires.

How to Develop Empathy:

Thankfully, we can relate to many experiences that others find themselves in, having lived through and experienced similar or identical events ourselves. Leaders leverage some of the skills referenced above in the "Making a Connection" chapter, which speak to actively looking for physiology, listening like a leader, interpreting the face value of words, and caring enough to deliberately probe for a sympathetic understanding that may elevate to empathy. A leader tries to allow themselves to feel what the other is feeling before making their next move.

If you're unable to distill another's feelings based on physiology, listening like a leader, and words presented, *ask* what the other party is feeling, and start by genuinely acknowledging those feelings.

Social Skills

Social skills speak to a leader's ability to confidently communicate effectively while instilling in others confidence and enthusiasm for change, using a wide range of skills. These leaders are able to successfully motivate others through their words and by example, having advanced insight into understanding their own feelings, and understanding the feelings of others, which better positions them to influence others. Leaders with social skills are not afraid to address negative comments or conflicts.

How to Develop Social Skills

These are varied and broad, but as they pertain to emotional intelligence, consider training in the areas of effective communication to improve your ability to influence beyond mere words and authority (this book and accompanying workshop!).

Consider studying conflict resolution that acknowledges potentially raw and heightened emotions, and the process of working toward mutually acceptable resolutions that honour the feelings of all involved (see "Emotional Intelligence as the Bridge Over an Impasse," later in this chapter, for an introduction).

Invest in learning how to create a happy environment via implementing a series of fun activities that you can rotate to stay fresh. These are breaks from the usual routine, higher stress days, intense seasons, or events like filing deadlines, beginning of the month madness, or living through an office renovation. You don't have to win a laugh-o-meter award here. Just try to let go of stress during a deliberate enforced pause, which acknowledges each other's presence *outside* of work during a shared chuckle.

Practice the social skill of giving effective praise. Using the social skill of praising, can lift the spirits of your team or collaborating peers, or it can confuse and discourage contributors if done incorrectly. When you offer the praise, *"You did a great job,"* it's confusing at best. What exactly did this person do that you are acknowledging and positively reinforcing? *"Thanks for staying back to help Sarah figure out how to key that invoice into the ABCD system. She's still learning, so I appreciate your contributions to her development and the teams' processing capacity,"* is much clearer about what behaviours you appreciate and want repeated. Be mindful of the authenticity of your praise. Praising lack-luster performance can discourage the actual heavy lifters on the team, and discredit you by bringing into question the authenticity of your praise for their legitimate praiseworthy work.

You may or may not feel that you already score high in emotional intelligence. There are different processes that I encourage clients to do in order to isolate and improve their emotional intelligence. It is possible to elevate your emotional intelligence and its effective application in *making a connection*. Like so many things, it takes commitment and some work, but the results will positively differentiate your contributions significantly.

*If you're interested in assessing your emotional intelligence, visit us at www.embracingleadershift.com for your exclusive access to a complementary Emotional Intelligence Assessment Tool and other bonus book materials.

Matters of the Heart – Acknowledging Emotions

There was a time when acknowledging your feelings or the feelings of others, and caring for each other in the workspace, was unheard of. We've progressed and better understand that emotions affect our commitment to people, ideas, how we influence each other, etc. To connect on an emotional level, you need to let your guard down. Essentially, you need to:

Be open – You need to allow people into your life if you expect them to invite you into theirs.

Be likable – People don't care what you know until they know that you care.

Come from a place of humility – Humility doesn't mean weakness or someone who thinks less of the value they bring, but rather someone who knows and uses their strengths for the benefit of others.

Be adaptable – Consider stepping into someone else's world for a while to get a better sense of their perspective, instead of expecting them to step into yours. Today, leaders don't know everything and aren't expected to. By empowering and leveraging those around you, new ways of solving problems and new ideas surface, which come from the diversity of life experiences and the knowledge of others.

Emotional Intelligence as the Bridge Over an Impasse

When you're attempting to influence someone's mindset or behavior and *meeting with resistance*, there are some common emotions that both sides are experiencing. Having the ability to identify and leverage shared emotions can be the first positive step toward establishing an emotional connection and the ultimate results you are aiming to achieve. For example, in a negotiation that is meeting with resistance, you can start off on the right foot by acknowledging that each collaborator appreciates being understood, and wants resolution to any conflict. Another shared emotion can be stress. Even though it can be felt differently, each individual is undergoing some level of stress until any conflict is resolved. You might highlight the shared emotions felt during what will be a challenging conversation, and express that you want the discussion to go well. Collaborators share the emotions around *good intentions*, as deliberators aren't usually aiming to hurt each other. There might be some shared emotions of frustration in not easily finding the words to express one's ideas, and to that point, you could express your appreciation for the commitment from your fellow collaborator in helping to identify and close any gaps in ideas being shared, etc. Having the ability to identify and leverage these emotions, support *making a connection*, as they convey transparency and trust building vulnerability, while creating additional common ground.

Two different individuals can achieve very different outcomes with the same group. One person can give a set of instructions or demands, and everyone nods their heads in unison but fails to take any significant action. Another person of equal or even lesser authority can ask for the same thing, and the whole team starts buzzing with activity and producing results above and beyond what is contractually required of them. Why the difference in the ability to influence and inspire the dramatically different outcome? One may have the title and more authority versus the other, but the difference in the ability to influence and inspire comes from *Making a Connection* with your target audience.

Let's look at where we are in the *Five Steps to Influence and Inspire Extraordinary Results*™: **Making a connection**, Building a Relationship, Establishing Trust, Casting a Vision, and Creating Buy-in. Let's read on to discover the importance of relationship building when influencing and inspiring others to extraordinary results.

*Visit us at www.embracingleadershift.com for your exclusive access to a complementary Emotional Intelligence Assessment Tool and other bonus book materials.

Reflection Pages

What ideas do I want to spend more time reflecting on, and how do they apply to me?

What can I do differently at work, home, or in the communities I serve, to help me grow and demonstrate my leadership?

Why am I doing this?

What does success look like after implementing these changes?

What is my target date to achieve that success?

What steps do I need to take in order to make these changes a reality?

What obstacles do I anticipate?

What resources will I need in people, services, tools, etc. in order to be successful?

How will I hold myself accountable to change and to my timeline?

Who will support me to ensure that what I imagine for myself becomes a reality?

Notes:

1   Mehrabian, A. Silent messages: Implicit Communication of Emotions and Attitudes. Belmont: Wadsworth. 2nd ed. Contemporary Psychology; 1981.
2   Lee D, Hatesohl D. Listening: Our Most Used Communications Skill. Missouri: MU Extension University of Missouri.
3   Kramer, R. *Leading by listening: An empirical test of Carl Rogers's theory of human relationship using interpersonal assessments of leaders by followers.* Doctoral dissertation, The George Washington University; 1997.
4   Mehrabian, A. Silent messages: Implicit Communication of Emotions and Attitudes. Belmont: Wadsworth; 1981.
5   Twaronite K, The Surprising Power of Simply Asking Coworkers How They're Doing. Harvard Business Review; 2019
6   Gallup. State of the American Manager. Wordpress.com; 2015
7   Volkema RJ. The Negotiation Toolkit: How to Get Exactly What You Want in Any Business or Personal Situation. United States of America: AMA Publications; 1999
8   Grobe M. In search of a common ground: How debate is bringing Europeans together. Europe: The Christian Science Monitor; 1999
9   Wikipedia; 2019

Chapter Six

Building Relationships

*"Everyone talks about building a relationship with your customer.
I think you build one with your employees first."*
– Angela Ahrendts (Former SVP Retail at Apple,
and CEO of Burberry)

*"Remember, don't let the pressure of doing business get in the way
of what doing business is truly about:
building relationships with people."*
– Rana el Kaliouby
(CEO of Affectiva – training robots to read feelings)

Five Steps to Influence and
Inspire Extraordinary Results™

Creating Buy-in

Casting a Vision

Establishing Trust

Building Relationships

Making a Connection

Building relationships in collaborative environments is an important part of being empowered to influence, inspire, and generate extraordinary results, whether you're the leader of a team or an individual leader among collaborating peers. In environments dependent on tapping into the group's diversity and, by extension, the diverse skills, experiences, ideas, and resulting creativity around solutions manufacturing, you need solid relationships that support a higher level of commitment and engagement to move initiatives forward. "Building Relationships" is the second step in the *Five Steps to Influence and Inspire Extraordinary Results*™. You no doubt will have heard the old adage that "people do business with people they know, like, and trust." Relationships speak to two of those qualifying factors; they give you a sense of who this person is, and whether you like them, based on what you feel, hear, and see. Trust is further along the *Five Steps to Influence and Inspire Extraordinary Results*™. Just because you've built a relationship with someone, it doesn't mean that you trust them, and more importantly, when you're aiming to influence others, that they trust you. We'll discuss *Establishing Trust*, in our next chapter. For now, let's focus on how to build a positive foundational relationship.

Be Genuinely Interested in Others

Who are you, and what unique talents do you bring? Leaders are wise to adopt this guiding mindset when engaging with others. As a leader, you should have a childlike curiosity that is determined to find out how this individual is superior to you in some way, given that they bring some knowledge, expertise, or experience that you don't, and as a leader, it's your job to find it. Dale Carnegie, the famous American writer and lecturer on self-improvement, salesmanship, and corporate training, has been quoted many times over for saying, *"You can make more friends in two months by becoming genuinely interested in other people, than you can in two years by trying to get other people interested in you,"* and in so doing, win their attention, time, and cooperation.[1] The more you show genuine interest in someone, their challenges in life, their philosophies, etc., the more interest they'll show in you. They'll want to talk to you, see you more, and entertain a relationship with you. It helps if you genuinely are curious about people. If you don't care to invest time to learn about what makes individuals unique, you have a bit of an uphill climb ahead of you.

Consider it your mission to see the world through someone else's eyes. You can't easily do this without a purposeful exploratory line of questioning. But if you can manage it, you can't help but convey your genuine interest, or at the very least, your honest effort to get to know them. Focus your attention on the speaker. Remember to use the leadership level of listening if you can, and be mindful that your physiology is accurately communicating the emotional message you are intending (or not intending) to convey. Always stop what you are doing, put down the mobile, and listen in, even if it's to acknowledge the request and schedule a better time to meet. If you're speaking to a direct report or a collaborating partner, and you're not keen on the topic they're sharing, or you are lost for words, try asking them, "What is it about XZY that's important to you?" or, "What will you do about it?" etc. If it's really painful to meet or seem interested in people, you need to do a bit of a self-check. This can be symptomatic of an underlying fear of rejection or not measuring up in some way, which creates social anxiety and insecurity. If this is the case, you have some additional work to do to overcome this.

Why is being interested in people so important to building positive relationships?

Getting people talking requires some effort, but the rewards are significant and are very real. Research tells us that when people talk about themselves, they generate activity in their brain's reward centres. Naturally, if you're speaking to them and encouraging the generation of those happy/rewarding feelings, they'll attribute those feelings to you and the existing or budding relationship. Researchers at Harvard University's Social Cognitive and Affective Neuroscience

Lab used functional magnetic resonating imaging (FMRI) to detect activity in the mesolimbic dopamine system of participants as they spoke. Participants spoke of others, themselves, to an audience, or privately. The area of the brain linked to pleasurable feelings and motivation associated with stimuli such as sex, cocaine, and good food, lit up most when individuals spoke of themselves and to an audience. [2] Is it any wonder why some of us find it so hard to resist speaking of ourselves, and is it any wonder that when you get such pleasurable feelings from someone, you tend to hold them in higher regard?

Smile, with Your Eyes

So now you're genuinely interested in getting to know people, or you're making a genuine effort, such that people will give you their time, attention, and cooperation as you work to build a relationship. And you understand the neuroscience of why taking the initiative puts you in a favourable position. You are well on your way—just a few more things to cover in relationship building. Next, remember to smile, with your eyes! As interacting human beings, generally speaking, smiles convey joy, happiness, sociability, and pleasure from someone's company. A smile generally signals that you are more likable and more approachable. Of course, in some cultures, smiling can mean very different things. In some cultures, excessive smiling can be seen as shallow or dishonest. In Asia, people smile to convey embarrassment or emotional pain. In the former Soviet Union, smiling at strangers in public was seen as suspicious behaviour! Rest assured, your audience will likely pick up the true essence of your smile and its genuine contribution to relationship building.

The French neurologist, Guillaume Duchenne, conducted research in the mid-19th century that identified two distinct types of smiles. A *Duchenne* smile involves the contraction of both the zygomatic major muscle that raises the corners of the mouth, and the orbicularis oculi muscle that raises the cheeks, to form "crow's feet" around the eyes.

Fake or *social* smiles are said to voluntarily contract the zygomatic major muscles around the mouth only, and are usually interpreted as inauthentic and forced. Face altering fans of Botox can be incorrectly categorized as fake or inauthentic, given their inability to move their orbicularis oculi muscles in their quest to be rid of "crow's feet." Dr. Paula Niedenthal's areas of research include emotion-cognition interaction, representational models of emotion, and the processing of facial expression. Dr. Niedenthal's research indicated that the person you are talking to is decoding your intentions by analysing the legitimacy of your smile in three ways. First, your audience is assessing the geometry of your face to a standard smile. Secondly, your audience is aware of the circumstances, and is sizing up the appropriateness of your smile to the situation. Finally, your audience will automatically mimic your smile, engaging the same muscles to attempt to generate the same feeling you are feeling as you speak, as a means to deciphering the authenticity of the smile! Dr. Niedenthal and her colleagues demonstrated this by impeding participants' ability to move *smiling muscles* while their partners spoke while smiling. Participants who were unable to mimic the smile they saw, and validate its authenticity, had a "much harder time telling which smiles were real and which were fake." [3] If you're building a relationship based on inauthenticity, know that your fake smile will give you away.

What's in a Name?

"That which we call a rose by any other name would smell as sweet."

You'll likely recognize this famous Shakespearian quote from Romeo and Juliet. Juliet tells Romeo that a name is an artificial and meaningless convention, and persuades him to give up his family name and be newly "baptised" as Juliet's lover. Most would suggest that Romeo is being very accommodating and is seriously motivated by the nature of the relationship he aims to pursue with Juliet. In his state, poor Romeo would agree to almost anything. But in business, what's in a name? *Everything*, according to Adam Alter, an Associate Professor of Marketing at New York University's Stern School of Business and Affiliate in the New York University Psychology Department. Alter points out several situations that speak to the importance and personal association that people make with their names, and why you need to get someone's name right when aiming to build a relationship. Alter writes that names are so important, there's evidence forecasting that two equally qualified recruits to a law firm, for example, will progress differently given their names. That is, the person with the simpler name (to the native language) will excel more readily, and that this is true among diverse groups and groups made up of white Anglo names. Our names come to have greater significance, and we are predisposed to hearing it.

The cognitive psychology phenomenon, known as the "cocktail party effect," would have us hear our name spoken across a room with 200 other noise making guests. We also develop an affinity for our own names. In varying countries, having varying alphabets, individuals prompted to circle their favorite letters will circle the letters in their name, 50% of the time. Donors to hurricane relief efforts are more likely to contribute when they share the same initial as the named storm! [4] Names are personal extensions of our sense of self, and are important. When someone abbreviates my name for their convenience, or calls me something like "Richard" instead of "Ricardo," my insides register the variance like a very low-grade seismic shift— subtle but detectable nonetheless. I like my name and feel a connection to it, as do most others. I know, names can be tough to remember. Here are a few tips to help you commit them to memory. And that's precisely where we'll start—commitment.

Commitment

Anyone can remember names. There are numerous tactics and references that offer tips and tricks, including those below; but ultimately, experts say that the number one indicator of your ability and success in remembering names boils down to your commitment to do the same. If you genuinely care about people and are willing to invest the time to get to know them, including their all-important name, you will meet with greater success and be well on your way to building the relationship. Stop blaming your bad memory. You may learn differently and, therefore, fare better, absorbing the information differently. Here are a few tactics and guiding principles. Consider trying some or all of them to see what works best for you.

Pay Attention

Ask and listen carefully for someone's name. If you're only asking for the sake of asking, or aren't really listening, or are distracted, you shouldn't expect to *hear it* or *register it,* much less remember it. If you missed it, just ask the person to repeat themselves, and if you still can't grasp it, ask them to spell it for you as you type it into your phone or write it down. This works if you're more of a visual learner. Are you being annoying? No, that person will sense that you are respectful and genuinely committed to getting it right—and won't they be impressed when you nail it and use it in conversation!

Use Their Name in Conversation

Ask them about the origin or the meaning of their name, if it's something unique. Sprinkle the use of their name throughout the conversation naturally, without overdoing it; this will help you commit the name to memory. When you say your goodbyes, use their name again!

Take Note

If you get a business card, write down details of your conversation on the back of the card to help you make the connection to the name. You can include anything prominent about how they look, dress, and speak, and any other details about their personal or professional life that they shared. Doing so will give you a persona for the name, and will also help you score relationship points for remembering details of your conversation the next time you meet. I keep my business card shipping boxes, and I fill them with collected business cards, divided by groups that I regularly interact with. Any time I can, I spend a few minutes reviewing those cards before attending an event, to help jog my memory about the people I'm about to visit with. My intention is to honor them and make them feel important by remembering their names and a few details about the last time we spoke.

Name Association

Play a game of name association. Try to find something about their name that relates in some way to the way they look or act etc., to create an image that offers you clues for their name. If you meet a "Star Reynolds," imagine her being "starry" eyed, looking at Burt "Reynolds" on the dance floor. If you meet a "Robert Long," and he happens to be tall, visualize the word, "LONG," written up the front of his long suit, or imagine him walking down the street with a famous actor, having a similar sounding name. Find a song that sounds like their name (proud "Mary" keep on burning; "Cecilia," you're breaking my heart), or make a rhyme that speaks to their name and any distinguishing behaviour, work, or unique physical traits (dapper Danny, flattering Fatima, roger that Roger, Peter peddles software, too tall Tony). You get the idea. Do what works for you. If this sounds like work… it is! If you want to win a contributor's attention, good will, and cooperation that comes with a relationship, you'll need to make the effort, and it will be worth it, because nothing rings as sweetly as the sound of one's own name.

The Attitude of Gratitude

Want a stronger relationship that endears people to you, and encourages more commitment and performance? Want to watch your relationships grow stronger while more and more people around you start repeatedly engaging positively with each other? Show appreciation and gratitude!

People appreciate being appreciated. And when you show them appreciation, don't be surprised when they start doing even better work, with greater commitment. Research out of the Wharton School at the University of Pennsylvania looked at two groups of students tasked to do the same activities, and found that the group thanked in advance for their efforts performed 50% better over the group who missed out on the appreciation.[5] Charles Schwab would agree. He said, "The way to develop the best that is in a person is by appreciation and encouragement." [6] Incidentally, Charles M. Schwab was an American steel magnate. Andrew Carnegie paid Charles $3000 a day, while someone well-off made $50 a week, to be president of United States Steel Company. This handsome salary wasn't for Schwab's incredible insights into the process of steel manufacturing; it was for his incredible insights into engaging with people.

Praising is Addictive

Why is showing appreciation or gratitude so important in engaging with people and strengthening relationships? Our hypothalamus controls bodily functions like sleep, eating, and the release of the neurotransmitter dopamine after being exposed to a rewarding stimulus like gratitude. The brain includes several distinct **dopamine** pathways, and one of these pathways plays a major role in the motivational component of reward-motivated behavior. As you read above, dopamine makes you feel good. So good in fact, many studies reference addictive behaviour in social media or gaming environments that are fuelled by the pleasure of dopamine release after generating *likes* on posts, or *awards* for reaching certain performance levels in a video game. This, of course, only motivates the person to generate even more likes or awards, in an on-going cycle of performance/dopamine generation reward. In his article, "The Grateful Brain, the neuroscience of giving thanks," Dr. Alex Korb indicates, *"Gratitude can have such a powerful impact on your life because it engages your brain in a virtuous cycle."* [7]

A virtuous cycle is a chain of events in which one desirable occurrence leads to another, which further promotes the first occurrence, and so on and so on, resulting in a continuous process of improvement. [8] This fact perpetuates a spirit of gratitude and a pay-it-forward mentality that could change the culture of an organization. Researchers have found that the pleasure inducing effects of a dopamine release are felt by both the individual giving the appreciation or gratitude, and by those receiving it. Hence, givers and receivers of appreciation feel good and are motivated to give out more and more appreciation in collaborative circles to generate more and more dopamine releases/rewards. This means a virtuous cycle of more and more positive messages of encouragement and recognition within the team. As a result, relationships are built and made stronger in a virtuous cycle.

What If the Praise Offered Is Insincere?

Let's talk about insincere praise or compliments also known as flattery, and how they impact building a relationship. These are compliments or praise often associated with manipulative behavior from someone who wants something. The flatterer will shower the flattered with insincere praise in order to generate positive feelings in the flattered, which predisposes them to do something nice for the flatterer in return. You would think most people would be wise enough to decipher mere flattery coming from someone who has obvious ulterior motives, and you'd be right! And you would think that seeing as how flattery is most often an obvious attempt to manipulate someone, that it wouldn't work, and you'd be wrong. Research done by Elaine Chan and Jaideep Sengupta, at the Hong Kong University of Science and Technology, showed that not only do individuals who miss the insincerity of a compliment accept the compliment, so do the individuals who know it's a lie. In their research, participants who were shown marketing material with outlandish flattery, held a retailer in higher regard than participants who were not exposed to the flattery. [9] Even though the outlandishly flattered participants were consciously aware and acknowledged the insincerity of compliments paid, this group showed better predictors of future purchases at the retailer, and an increased likelihood of joining the retailer's shopper's program. How could this be? The research suggests that we usually view ourselves in high esteem due to the *above average phenomenon*. We generally believe that we are above average at everything, even though, statistically, it's not possible. Nonetheless, we want to believe that the compliment is accurately paid, and part of our subconscious actually believes it and more readily accepts any information that further promotes the ingrained belief. The conscious mind might see the insincerity immediately, but it will take several contradicting experiences to finally convince the subconscious mind to change its securely held belief paradigm. The study also demonstrated that individuals who were more often accepting of flattery were individuals in need of an emotional pick-me-up.

Praising with Integrity

Flattery might work to persuade subordinates or collaborating peers to whom the compliments were paid, and have a positive effect on your ability to influence them, build a relationship with them, and even predispose them to do something nice for you, especially if they need an emotional pick-me-up. But be forewarned of the negative side of flattery that's used to manipulate people. Without even getting into a conversation about moral standards, people in and around, who hear a flatterer's insincere compliments that are not directed at them, and hence aren't "blinded" by a subconscious mind that is predisposed to agree with an outlandish compliment, will likely think less of the manipulator. The other subordinates or collaborating peers will find the flatterer less reliable in their ability to pass along accurate feedback, and going forward will take any feedback with a grain of salt. The lack of trustworthiness comes as people view the false praise as a form of deception. As a result, the flatterer has actually hindered their ability to reap the many rewards that come from honest appreciation or praise, and the relationship it helps to build.

Praising with Specificity

The same holds true for inaccurate praise that holds true for false praise. People in and around inaccurately placed praise will be less likely to accept future well-intending praise, or to reap the intended rewards, as these people will again take every compliment with a grain of salt. When you're giving praise, be accurate. As the leader of a team or as an individual leader among collaborating peers, it's important to be clear about what behaviour you're recognizing and, therefore, want repeated. Loose comments, like "Great job," or "That went well," are uplifting but confusing. The person receiving the praise will aim to repeat *everything* they just did next time round, to keep the badge of honor. Now they're trapped. There is always room for improvement, but given that this individual doesn't know exactly what they did well, and what perhaps was done moderately well, their performance is doomed to stop improving. Better feedback might include, "Great job on monitoring our progress through the itinerary during the meet this morning; thank you for keeping us on schedule," or, "You answered most of the questions thrown at you to the satisfaction of everyone at the table; I appreciate the effort you put into preparing for the group," or, "Thanks for staying back to help Sara with imputing this month's data into Data-Vault; I appreciate you supporting her development and the future capacity of this team." On occasion, the feedback you need to share as a leader isn't always positive.

Feedback Isn't Always Praise

What happens when a leader of a team, or an individual leader among collaborating peers, takes exception to how someone is contributing, and feels they need to correct the behaviour with what is often referred to as criticism? A collaborator might think that the criticism they offer is merely well-intending advice or instruction. Many managers feel they must criticize as a necessary part of their job to enhance performance, as this helps the criticized person address dysfunctional habits that impede their effectiveness. Tread carefully, and here's why. When someone judges your work or abilities as wanting, it can be demoralizing, creates anger, defiance, secretiveness, and withdrawal. This then causes the person judging to feel that the negative judgment is increasingly justified, and it compels them to criticize even more. This is followed by more separation, resentment, defiance, and withdrawal, and so goes the vicious negative relationship-destroying cycle.

Some people deliberately criticize for the unconstructive purpose of stroking their own ego, or find fault and lash out at others merely in an attempt to make themselves look superior or console deeply held insecurity. We've all met the office bully whose criticisms contradict themselves almost on a weekly basis, and who seem to go into aphylactic shock when they have to compliment you, or someone compliments you in their presence. This type of criticism is destined to damage relationships and productivity. Dr. Richard Boyatzis, from the University of Weatherhead School of Management, conducted research that interviewed participants who positively focussed on dreams and goals, and then participants who negatively focussed on what you should do to fix yourself. The brain scans revealed that the positive interview elicited activity in reward circuitry and areas for good memories and upbeat feelings, while the negative interview lit up areas related to anxiety, sadness, and worrying. [10] Dr. Daniel Goleman, the American psychologist who first popularized emotional intelligence, wrote the article, "When you criticize someone, you make it harder for that person to change." He notes, *"that line of thinking puts us on defense, and narrows our possibilities to rescue operations."* This is the difference between mind-opening queries versus conversations about what's wrong with you and what you need to fix.[11]

Be Positive

As the leader of a group, or as a well intending individual leader among collaborating peers, focussing on the positive will support someone's accelerated development and their ability to come up with more viable options, as opposed to focussing on the negative. Dr. Barbara Frederickson, a psychologist at the University of North Carolina, found that "positive feelings enlarge the aperture of our attention to embrace a wider range of possibility and... motivate(s) us to work toward a better future." [12] Dr. Goleman suggests that being in a positive mood activates brain circuits that remind us of how good it feels to hit a goal. This encourages us to work on smaller steps in a project, or on our behaviour along the way. This circuitry runs on pleasure inducing dopamine and endogenous opioids, and as Dr. Goleman suggests, staying positive pays off in our performance. Dr. Frederickson indicates that staying positive energizes us, improves focus, flexible thinking, and helps us connect more effectively with people around us. [13]

The Essence of Coaching

It's been suggested that judging someone is really a protest against others who would dare to do things differently from ourselves. This is a trap that coaches can fall into when they are attempting to *mentor* versus *coach* a subordinate or collaborating partner. What worked for a *mentor* back in their heyday, might not work today. The world, the economy, technology, and group dynamics are constantly changing, and even the mentor might find it more difficult to succeed leveraging an old strategy that no longer resonates. A well-intending *mentor,* no doubt, has many fine qualities and strengths, but the individual they are mentoring surely possesses a different combination of them. A *coach* would encourage an individual to play to their strengths, and there is much research to confirm that this is far more motivating and supportive of the much sought-after *engagement* that organizations are looking for today. A *coach* should create awareness via questioning, and encourage an individual to brainstorm options that would come far more readily in a positive frame of mind, as we have seen above. A *coach* should guide the conversation to encourage "enlarging the aperture" of options by asking, in the spirit of progress and lacking in any judgment, what the individual thought went favourably, and what might be some options they could try in the future to push the needle still further. If time is of the essence, or the individual being coached doesn't have the experience to weigh in significantly, then a *coach* might try a "feedback sandwich" that includes healthy amounts of positive observations at the front and tail end of the conversation, and recommendations for enhancements that might support their ongoing success, "sandwiched" in the middle. Most everyone is doing something right; as a leader of a team or as an individual leader collaborating among peers, you need to find it and bring it to light. The relationship will prosper, as will the effectiveness of the collaboration. A strong relationship is the precursor to establishing trust, and trust is the topic of our next chapter and next step in our leader's engagement process.

Reflection Pages

What ideas do I want to spend more time reflecting on, and how do they apply to me?

What can I do differently at work, home, or in the communities I serve, to help me grow and demonstrate my leadership?

Why am I doing this?

What does success look like after implementing these changes?

What is my target date to achieve that success?

What steps do I need to take in order to make these changes a reality?

What obstacles do I anticipate?

What resources will I need in people, services, tools, etc. in order to be successful?

How will I hold myself accountable to change and to my timeline?

Who will support me to ensure that what I imagine for myself becomes a reality?

Notes:

1 Carnegie D, Carnegie DD. How to Win Friends & Influence People. Revised edition, New York, United States of America: Gallery Books; 1981

2 Ward AF. The Neuroscience of Everybody's Favorite Topic: Why do people spend so much time talking about themselves? SCIENTIFIC AMERICAN: scientificamerican.com; 2013

3 Widrich L. The Science of Smiling: A Guide to The World's Most Powerful Gesture.buffer.com: Buffer; 2016

4 Alter A. What's in a Name? Everything. Bigthink.com: BIG THINK; 2013

5 Tanner OC. The Psychological Effects of Workplace Appreciation & Gratitude. emergenetic.com: emergenetics INTERNATIONAL; 2014

6 Carnegie D, Carnegie DD. How to Win Friends & Influence People. Revised edition, New York, United States of America: Gallery Books; 1981

7 Korb A. The Grateful Brain: The neuroscience of giving thanks. Psychologytoday.com: Psychology Today; 2012

8 Merriam-Webster Dictionary. Merriam-webster.com; 2019

9 Valdesolo P. Flattery Will Get You Far: Even obviously manipulative compliments are remarkably effective. Scientificamerican.com: SCIENTIFIC AMERICAN; 2010

10 Goleman D. When You Criticize Someone, You Make It Harder for That Person to Change. hbr.org: Harvard Business Review; 2013

11 Ibid.

12 Ibid.

13 Ibid.

Chapter Seven

Establishing Trust

*"If we can by any method establish a relation of mutual trust
between the laborer and the employer,
we shall lay the foundation stone of a structure
that will endure for all time."*
– Mark Hanna (former United States Senator)

*"Earn trust, earn trust, earn trust.
Then you can worry about the rest."*
– Seth Godin (American multiple bestselling author)

Five Steps to Influence and
Inspire Extraordinary Results™

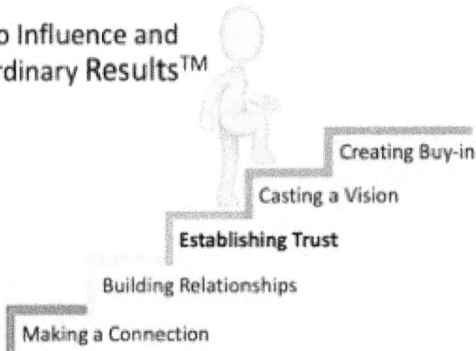

Creating Buy-in

Casting a Vision

Establishing Trust

Building Relationships

Making a Connection

The Merriam-Webster Dictionary describes trust as the certainty or security generated by the reliance on the character, ability, strength, or truth of someone or something. The absence of trust in organizations manifests fear, and left unchecked, people in organizations spend time debating roles and responsibilities, don't share information, point fingers at others in an effort to protect themselves and their interests, and generate lack luster performance. When trust is present, individuals in organizations feel safe knowing that they can count on each other to have the character to do the right thing and be accountable for their actions without fear. With trust, individuals support each other as they take calculated risks without fear of persecution for making a mistake. Trust creates a sense of safety with the leader of a team or within individual leaders among collaborating peers. With trust comes the absence of fear and uncertainty, and the much-coveted innovation, creativity, collaboration, and productivity that organizations aspire to. Trust is a necessary and important step in the *Five Steps to Influence and Inspire Extraordinary Results*™.

Many things of great value require time and effort to bring something powerful or remarkable to fruition, and trust is no exception. And yet, like any precious art piece representing hours or years of concentrated effort, trust can be lost in an instant, or depreciate incrementally if neglected. You cannot take people, and the trust established with them, for granted, and expect trust to still be there without consistent words, and more importantly, consistent action to sustain it.

Trust Beneficiaries

Paul J. Zak is an American neuroeconomist and Harvard researcher. He is the founding director of the Center for Neuroeconomics Studies, and Professor of Economics, Psychology and Management at Claremont Graduate University, and has invested decades researching the neurological connection between trust, leadership, and organizational performance. Zak and his team found that "compared with people at low-trust companies, people at high-trust companies report 74% less stress, 106% more energy at work, 50% higher productivity, 13% fewer sick days, 76% more engagement, 29% more satisfaction with their lives, and 40% less burnout." [1]

Trust the Science

Zak hypothesized that a neurological signal in the brain contributed to one's ability to trust someone, leveraging research done on rodents, where it was found that a brain chemical called *oxytocin* signalled that another animal was safe to approach. His research in the lab, in thousands of companies, and as far away as the rain forest of Papua, New Guinea, showed that the relationship between oxytocin and trust was universal and consistent in humans. Given the production of oxytocin in the brain, which causes trust, and supports such favorable results indicated above, you must be eager to learn what produces such an effect, and I'm eager to share. The following are avenues to stimulating the production of the trust chemical, *oxytocin,* with your team. Each recommendation will include an aspect of Zak's research that validates that the recommendations work according to seasoned leaders and neuroscience.

Transparency and Integrity

Research tells us that less than half of employees are well informed of their company's goals, plans, priorities, opportunities, strategies, etc. This lack of information sharing often leads to stress, relating to the uncertainty of where the company is headed, the shallow understanding of the market it operates in, and the insecurity of longer-term employment. Zak's research found that stress inhibits the release of the trust building chemical, oxytocin, in the brain, and that the *antidote* is openness. As a leader of a team, or individual leader among collaborating peers, it's critical that you share important or relevant information immediately. This includes information about the financial performance of the company. Communicating openly will signal that you don't have a hidden agenda and will encourage others to do the same. Doing this creates a culture based on trust, where employees feel comfortable speaking honestly and in a more meaningful way about progress to plan and challenges they are encountering, while encouraging participation in joint problem-solving collaboration.

Don't stretch the truth. When you are caught in a lie, it invariably diminishes the trust people have in you. The effort it will take to win back that trust will be ten times the effort you were trying to avoid with what you thought was a harmless fib. You may think the little lie was harmless, but you are putting colleagues or subordinates on guard to scrutinize what comes out of your mouth more closely, or just dismiss you altogether as untrustworthy. Be true to your word by keeping the promises you've made to your team, and if you're unsure as to your ability to deliver anything, don't promise to do it. Say what you mean, and mean what you say. If you indicate that there will be consequences for certain behaviour, or that "this is the last time we'll have to work this hard to meet a deadline," you better mean it and follow through; otherwise you'll find collaborators not responding when you really need them, because they have heard unfulfilled proclamations one too many times. You must walk the talk in all things, and be willing to adopt any standards you set for others; otherwise the trust and your credibility will suffer, as will the support for your new standard.

Openly discuss your team and/or personal values, and defend them. Teams benefit from clear direction regarding acceptable behaviour and guiding principles. Don't abandon or sacrifice those values in search of approval, as individuals around you will notice. You may have to say no on occasion and create some temporary conflict, but longer term, collaborators will respect your integrity and appreciate your consistency. Your team's trust in you will grow as they witness that your actions are guided by what you feel is the right thing to do, not what you think others want to see or hear.

Give Trust to Get Trust

This can be done in a number of ways as the leader of a team or individual leader among collaborating peers, by demonstrating trust in others. This includes the rest of your team, your boss, the executive, and even demonstrating trust in yourself. Your team is always watching you; make sure you are demonstrating the commitment and benefits of trusting others. This can sometimes be difficult when you are supporting the growth of someone who has previously disappointed you. After a quick check-in regarding the task at hand and the competence required, you have to give people the benefit of the doubt and let them try again. Failing to trust them stagnates their growth and damages your leadership example of trusting others. As a leader, you should give the assistance that is required of you, then let your team execute. If you're supervising others, nothing destroys establishing trust like micromanaging your team. By hovering over your employees or constantly checking in on what they're doing, you are consciously or unconsciously conveying a lack of trust in that employee's ability to complete the work or manage their time. To avoid this trust damaging effect, consider prescheduling spaced out updates or check-ins to oversee the completion of work, from more of a distance.

Give away your authority. Like passing over the keys to your new ride to your teenager, this inspires team members to step up their game and seek to demonstrate that the trust was well placed. There are any number of tasks or responsibilities that can be shared or rotated among team members. This can include regular meetings, where the agenda and leading the meeting itself can be *entrusted* to someone else. Consider delegating decision making to the team, on key aspects of what needs to be done on a project or event. Delegating parts of your authority to the team will exemplify what trust looks like, and will generate the positive statistics described above. Let the team decide *how to* execute the project. Research done by Citigroup and LinkedIn found that almost half of employees would give up a 20% raise for greater control over how they worked.[2] This is a great way to promote creativity and innovation, in that different employees bring the strength of diversity, having different life and work experiences, and with it, variation in recommendations for execution that may vary significantly from yours. Letting individuals decide where they will contribute, based on their strengths, is also a great way to get results and build trust with key individuals who lend their strengths in targeted areas, rather than demanding that someone with lesser expertise shoulder the burden. In fact, Zak's research confirmed giving discretion as to how work was done, and enabling employees to craft their own jobs generates oxytocin in the brain and the subsequent trust it creates.[3]

Demonstrating the certainty or security generated by the reliance on the character, ability, strength, or truth of someone or something, means relaxing constrictive rules and processes that hinder progress with individuals and within organizations. Your team for the most part are competent, creative adults, helping you generate value; hence, they should be trusted to perform without the constraints of a heavy rule book. Excessive rules and procedures stifles creativity and action. There will always be an element of risk in making yourself vulnerable by giving your trust to your team while working together toward something of importance, but in accepting the calculated risk, oxytocin is triggered in the target audience, and trust is established. Let's look at another way to generate trust and the subsequent rewards.

Recognize Contributions

Remember to give praise and recognize excellence at every legitimate praiseworthy moment. This will cast you in a light of selfless generosity as you acknowledge the power and competence in others, instead of taking it for yourself. Flexing your leadership muscle by putting others in the spotlight when things go well, and placing them behind the curtain when things don't, will nurture trusting collaborators who will repay you many times over. If you make the mistake of only highlighting errors, you will find that your team will evolve into a group where enterprising risk takers leave, and people who are fearful and play small, stay. So, when is the most effective time to offer legitimate praise to help generate oxytocin and the trust it produces? According to Zak's research, *"The neuroscience shows that recognition has the largest effect on trust when it occurs immediately after a goal has been met, when it comes from peers, and when it's tangible, unexpected, personal, and public."* [4]

Discourage the shaming and blaming that sometimes happens when inevitably something goes wrong or a mistake was made. Allowing finger pointing at one another will quickly create a toxic culture that erodes trust. Instead, strive to make every "mistake" a learning opportunity, where the team comes together to clearly define what went wrong, what the outcome was, what can be done to prevent a reoccurrence, and if you're lucky, what the silver lining was in this misstep. Did this smaller misstep allow for the creation of firewalls that now prevent far greater issues down the road and, while disruptive, may have been a blessing in disguise? And if nothing else, the misstep likely tested the collaborative strength of the team's mettle in enduring, reacting, and solving the challenge together, which is one more thing to celebrate and recognize.

One final note on recognition, as the leader of a team or as an individual leader among collaborating peers: be careful not to belittle anyone or their performance, or make them feel incompetent. Such condescension or contempt will erode trust. However, as a leader, you still need to hold individuals accountable for their actions and subsequent outcomes. Failing to hold individuals accountable to their performance, or lack thereof, will lessen your credibility and your efforts to build trust with the balance of the watching team.

Show Your Vulnerability

Some might see purposefully conveying dependency, or mistakes, in order to establish trust, as manipulative. Not so, if you're conveying vulnerability for the purpose of encouraging others to learn and reach for targets that the group sometimes misses. This signals to your team or collaborating peers that this is a safe place to admit missteps, as you are readily admitting you've done the same. Sleep soundly, knowing your integrity is solid and that you are on your way to establishing trust. As a leader, you are your own public relations department, and as one of my former performance coaches once told me when I managed a larger team, it does your reputation no good to go out of your way to demonstrate your supportive character if no one takes notice. Make the effort for the right reason, *and* get visibility.

Make yourself vulnerable by asking for the help when collaborating on projects. Research shows that asking for help, and admitting that you don't know everything, shows vulnerability and helps build trust. Zak's research team found that "Leaders in high-trust workplaces ask for help from colleagues instead of just telling them to do things. …. this stimulates oxytocin production in others increasing their trust and cooperation. Asking for help is a sign of a secure leader—one who engages everyone to reach goals."[5] When you and your collaborating peers pitch in together, it also creates a vulnerability to each other, as each contributor depends on the other to check each other's work or make their unique contribution to the whole. Each collaborator is at some risk when the outcome of the project is seen as a joint success or misstep. However, trust is built when your team or collaborating peers have the opportunity to disappoint you or hurt you, and don't.

We discussed the reality that not all performances can be recognized as positive; to establish trust with your team, if a *mistake* was yours, you need to own it. Everyone makes mistakes, and when you try to hide yours, your subordinates or collaborating peers will perceive you as dishonest, and your trustworthiness will erode. If you admit your error or lack of insight, you're signalling to the balance of the team that if you don't know this or anything else in the future, you'll just admit it and not try to fake it; hence, they can trust what comes out of your mouth. Use your mistake to teach others, and ask for feedback from the group. Be sure to use the feedback where you can; genuinely thank the collaborators who provided the valuable feedback, and let them know how you used it.

Be Human

Treat others like the unique individuals deserving of respect that they are. Strive to demonstrate this when making decisions that also include dollars and cents or operational efficiencies. When you put people first, they'll believe that you hold them in higher regard and will trust that you have their back, and in return, they'll have yours. Often, the balanced solution that honors people and fiscal objectives just requires additional creativity. Finally, express vulnerability by using that human side in your communications as well. Drop the formality in communications that can sometimes build a wall between the author and the reader. The formality may not be your reader's preferred style of communication, and it isolates them from you, eroding that vulnerable human connection and trust. This is harder than it sounds; I'm not a trained writer or language aficionado by any means, but I too have been known to lay it on pretty thick when I'm writing to impress.

Be Altruistic

Giving of yourself, your time, and your energy to others, without expectations of reward, is another way to generate trust. Authentic kindness builds trust because individuals see the well intending effort that you have put into developing others, without a hidden agenda. If you genuinely want only good things for others, and make a point to consistently demonstrate this, people will come to trust that everything you do will reflect this truth about you. Your altruistic acts will create a halo effect on everything you do. One way to build trust this way is by investing effort to understand the career aspirations of individuals you supervise. Help your subordinates build or refine skills that will position them to perform well in their current roles, as well as prepare them for their next one. Don't be afraid to flat out ask individuals what you can do to help them progress. The response may surprise you, and may actually ask very little of you as a supervisor. Asking flat out takes the burden off a supervisor to guess how hard to push, and to guess what kind of progress would create the greatest sense of satisfaction.

If you're working on a collaborative team and have some discretion as to how to advance projects, work with peers to understand gaps in development and design project roles that help your peers fill those gaps. Be deliberate about how each of you are contributing, and take on opportunities to stretch talents that can later be added to a résumé. Investing selflessly to understand someone's development goals, and supporting them in achieving them, is a good way to establish trust. Zak's research confirms that the oxytocin generating organizations that rank high in trust are more inclined to adopt this altruistic practice, over low trust organizations. Zak reports, "High-trust companies adopt a growth mindset when developing talent. Some even find that when managers set clear goals, give employees the autonomy to reach them, and provide consistent feedback, the backward-looking annual performance review is no longer necessary. Instead, managers and direct reports can meet more frequently to focus on professional and personal growth.[6]

Personal development can also be done on a larger scale in team building activities. I'm not talking about poorly planned activities that are more about having fun and generating temporary effects in terms of *happiness* or *satisfaction* at work, which does nothing to improve trust, build relationships, or improve retention or performance. Team activities should have clearly defined objectives that are understood by all participants. Events should encourage healthy competition, with challenging tasks, but be lighthearted and something that everyone can participate in. Always go over the takeaways and lessons learned with the participants to make sure the connection was made between the activity and the purpose (in this case, help establish trust).

The challenge need not be outside the office. There are great benefits to introducing activities or challenges that promote working together, which sharpen the team's focus and establishes trust. Zak's neuroscience research indicates, inducing a *challenge stress* releases neurochemicals, including oxytocin and adrenocorticotropin, which intensifies people's focus, and strengthens social connections. Consider assigning the team a difficult but achievable job, having moderate stress. Be guided by the SMART* goal planning process when planning the group challenge, just as you might when planning an individual challenge. Zak's research found that "this works only if challenges are attainable and have a concrete end point; vague or impossible goals cause people to give up before they even start. Leaders should check in frequently to assess progress and adjust goals that are too easy or out of reach." [7]

*For a SMART Goal Checklist that you can use to plan your group or individual challenge, visit us at www.embracingleadershift.com for your exclusive access to this and other bonus book materials.

The neuroscience supports what seasoned leaders know to be true: Establishing trust is nonnegotiable for leaders of teams or individual leaders working among collaborating peers. No trust equals poor traction on initiatives; so, trust is an integral part of the leader's engagement process, the *Five Steps to Influence and Inspire Extraordinary Results*[TM]. High trust companies generate the kind of results listed above in productivity, energy at work, collaboration, lower attrition, less stress, etc., and when you are more productive and more innovative in a competitive labor market, you can generate the difference in salaries between high trust and low trust companies that Zak and his team discovered. The more innovative, more productive, high trust companies, on average, pay their employees 17% more than lower trust company employees.[8] It would seem that membership, in a trust culture, has its privileges too.

*Visit us at www.embracingleadershift.com for your exclusive access to the SMART Goal Checklist and other bonus book materials.

Five Steps to Influence and Inspire Extraordinary Results™

Creating Buy-in
Casting a Vision
Establishing Trust
Building Relationships
Making a Connection

Use this *SMART Goal Format – Checklist* when setting goals for yourself or for your team challenges to ensure that the activities you create to *Establish Trust* are well organized and productive

Advanced Leadership

SMART Goal Format - Checklist		
Specific	Is the goal clearly articulated? Does the goal require collaboration from others? Is it clear who needs to accomplish each contributing piece? What will you contribute or do exactly?	Yes / No
Measurable	Does the goal answer the question of how many? How often? What will you reference as a measure of your progress / success?	Yes / No
Achievable	Do you have access to the resources you need? Are the resources you need available to you, at the right time, to ensure you meet your target date? Are the forecasted results realistic?	Yes / No
Relevant	Will this goal enhance your well-being? Will this goal enhance your career progression? Will this goal improve your business significantly? Will this goal support important relationships you value?	Yes / No
Time-bound	Does the goal specify a clear and specific completion date and or identify milestones along the way?	Yes / No

Reflection Pages

What ideas do I want to spend more time reflecting on, and how do they apply to me?

What can I do differently at work, home, or in the communities I serve, to help me grow and demonstrate my leadership?

Why am I doing this?

What does success look like after implementing these changes?

What is my target date to achieve that success?

What steps do I need to take in order to make these changes a reality?

What obstacles do I anticipate?

What resources will I need in people, services, tools, etc. in order to be successful?

How will I hold myself accountable to change and to my timeline?

Who will support me to ensure that what I imagine for myself becomes a reality?

Notes:

1   Zak P. The Neuroscience of Trust. Hbt.org: Harvard Business Review; 2017
2   Citigroup Inc. The Career Peak Paradox: New Citi/LinkedIn Survey Suggests Professionals Believe Success is a Moving Target. Citigroup.com: Citi; 2014
3   Zak P. The Neuroscience of Trust. Hbt.org: Harvard Business Review; 2017
4   Ibid.
5   Ibid.
6   Ibid.
7   Ibid.
8   Ibid.

Chapter Eight

Casting a Vision

"Leadership is having a compelling vision, a comprehensive plan, relentless implementation, and talented people working together."
– Alan Mulally (American engineer, former president and CEO of the Ford Motor Company. He was included in the 2009 *Time 100* list, due to his achievements at Ford.)

"Good business leaders create a vision, articulate a vision, passionately own the vision, and relentlessly drive it to completion.
– Jack Welch, former chairman and CEO at General Electric (During his 1981–2001 tenure at GE, the company's value rose by an incredible 4,000%, making it the most valuable corporation in the world at one time.)

Five Steps to Influence and
Inspire Extraordinary Results™

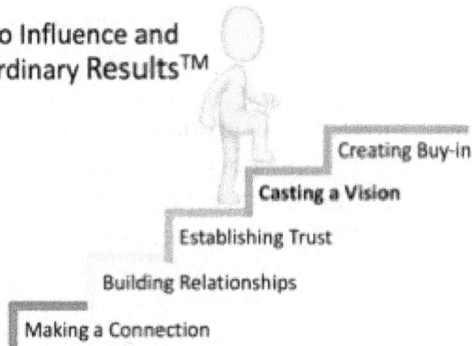

Creating Buy-in

Casting a Vision

Establishing Trust

Building Relationships

Making a Connection

Martin Luther King Jr. had a mission and belief that his children and others could live in a world of equals. He communicated some pretty high expectations to his followers, who would put themselves in harm's way to do what he asked of them. Martin Luther King Jr. managed to persuade over 200,000 people to go out onto the streets of Washington, in 1963. He did this long before anyone could tweet out a message or post to Facebook, "The struggle is real; meet me at the Lincoln memorial." People will give a leader what is contractually required of them, but people will give a leader blood, sweat, and tears when a leader inspires them. Mr. King did just that. He inspired followers by vividly describing an alternate world that moved people to follow him, not because he had all the answers or a list of things that needed to be done to ensure success. He famously proclaimed, "I have a dream," not, "I have a plan." King engaged emotions and literally inspired contributions of blood, sweat, and tears, or *discretionary effort*, with a powerful vision of the future he imagined. As the son of a Baptist Pastor, King Jr. likely knew, or intuitively knew, that a vision should be compelling, a little bit inspirational, and help people feel a sense of pride as they come to know that they're part of a movement or organization that's moving toward something bigger, something better.

A Vision Statement Should...

The current predominantly millennial workforce embraces the idea of contributing with purpose, and are less attracted to money as a motivating factor, compared to previous generations. Communicating a vision that motivates and conveys a purpose that people can emotionally connect to, beyond "making money," has become much more important and has received a greater sense of urgency more recently. Leveraging emotions is crucial when casting a vision in an effort to influence, inspire, and generate extraordinary results, as the leader of a team or as individual leaders among collaborating peers. We'll discuss the importance of emotions in casting a vision, in greater detail, later in the chapter. A vision statement should serve as a beacon that guides individuals in an organization, along an inspired path to a vividly defined aspirational future, to ensure that contributions are future focussed and proactive, instead of merely reactive to current market conditions. A vision statement should stand the test of time and not require revisions after every change in the organization's leadership, or in response to passing business fads. Finally, a vision statement should be simply stated and easy to remember. Every effort up front, to simplify the message, will be rewarded with instant comprehension and the creation of message sharing ambassadors. The role of the leader(s) in the construction of the vision statement is to help extract a vision statement that speaks to the intrinsic DNA of an organization—it cannot be created; it is found.

Vision Benefits

There are many benefits to casting a solid vision when attempting to influence, inspire, and generate extraordinary results. In a world full of unrelenting change and unknowns, an organization may not know *what* will be required to be successful in the future, but with a well-crafted vision statement, they know *how* they will approach that unknown future. That is, in terms of consistently applied values and shared purpose, etc. Having a future-state vision supports goal setting in organizations seeking a bright future, as opposed to organizations who don't see the value in drafting one, and are left with floundering, aimless, independent silos that sometimes hinder each other's success when they can't see a common future. Solid vision statements provide a shared destination, and encourage a workforce to creatively solve their own problems instead of waiting to be told what to do. These groups have greater independence via confidence inspiring sightlines into where the organization is headed. A solid vision statement is also a benefit in helping highly skilled talent feel like they belong to something greater than themselves. This helps with retention while attracting like-minded, equally skilled talent. A well-crafted vision statement lessens a workforce's anxiety that comes from employment insecurity born of constant change in and around them. A vision statement signals that despite change, the organization sees a future and envisions themselves contributing to it.

Confusion in Terminologies

When we speak of "vision," there is some confusion, given the variety of associations and meanings assigned to the word. The Oxford Dictionary supports this with a long list of associated synonyms, including: imagination, creativity, creative power, inventiveness, innovation, inspiration, intuition, perceptiveness, perception, breadth of view, foresight, insight, far-sightedness, prescience, discernment, awareness, penetration, shrewdness, sharpness, and cleverness! There are also a multitude of vision statement formation processes that create varying results. Some of the confusion comes from the way people use terms interchangeably, like mission, vision, strategy, values, goals, etc. Some definitions of *vision* include numerical measures of success and time bound deadlines for completion. However, these are better communicated in business plans and business goals, which represent current activities contributing to manifesting the future vision.

How to Write a Vision Statement

I studied a number of models, looking for a simple formula that was easy to understand and replicate when drafting a vision statement. I wanted something with the functionality of filling in a few boxes to create a message. I also wanted something that spoke to eliciting an emotional response from the audience a leader was aiming to influence, inspire, and generate extraordinary results with. Finally, I wanted something that was more than just a collection of ideas; I wanted supporting research that proved the process would work. In my research, I found the work of James C. Collins and Jerry I. Porras, who spent time understanding the power of casting a vision while researching and writing, *Built to Last: Successful Habits of Visionary*

Companies. The list of companies included in their study are titans like Disney, 3M, Sony, Proctor and Gamble, Johnson and Johnson, and Hewlett-Packard, to name a few. Collectively, the study's group were visionaries who outperformed the general stock market **by a factor of 12,** since 1925. Collins and Porras's guidance around building a vision statement, outlined in their Harvard Business Review article, showcased the knowledge they gained from working with such an impressive group.[1] Their recommendation met my search for a simple formula that's easy to replicate, elicits emotion, and has the research and results over time to confirm that it works.

Here is the Collin and Porras process for creating a Vision Statement:

Vision = Core Ideology + Envisioned Future

Where:

Core Ideology = Core Values + Core Purpose

and

Envisioned Future = Big Hairy Audacious Goal (BHAG) + a Vivid Description

The authors describe **Core Ideology** (Core Values + Core Purpose) as a company's timeless character and holdfast, while the company's business strategies and practices adapt to the changing world.

Core Values are described as "the handful of guiding principles by which a company navigates. They require no external justification."[2]

The following example is provided: "Disney's core values of imagination and wholesomeness stem from the founder's belief that these should be nurtured for their own sake, not merely to capitalize on a business opportunity."[3] So committed were these organizations to their core values, that if their core values and markets conflicted, they would pursue new markets before changing their core values.

Core Purpose is described as "an organization's most fundamental reason for being. It should not be confused with the company's current product lines or customer segments. Rather, it reflects people's idealistic motivations for doing the company's work."[4]

The following example is provided: "Disney's core purpose is to make people happy, not to build theme parks and make cartoons."[5]

The authors describe **Envisioned Future** (Big, Hairy, Audacious Goals: BHAGs + Vivid Descriptions) as a "10–30-year audacious goal plus a vivid description of what it would be like to achieve that goal."[6]

Big, Hairy, Audacious Goals – BHAGs are described as tangible, energizing, and highly focussed. It has a bold and easy-to-identify finish line that the company can shoot for and likely achieve with great effort and a little luck. They should be simple to remember, and shouldn't require a wordsmithing committee.

For example, NASA's 1960s mission to the moon, inspired by President John F. Kennedy, had a clear vision: landing a man on the moon and returning him safely to the earth by the end of the decade.

Vivid Description is described as "a vibrant, engaging, and specific description of what it would be like to achieve the BHAG. Think of it as translating the vision from words into pictures, of creating an image that people can carry around in their heads."[7]

The following example is provided: "Henry Ford brought to life the goal of democratizing the automobile, with this vivid description: I will build a motorcar for the great multitude... it will be so low in price that no man making a good salary will be unable to own one and enjoy with his family the blessing of hours of pleasure in God's great open spaces... When I'm through, everybody will be able to afford one, and everyone will have one. The horse will have disappeared from our highways, the automobile will be taken for granted... [and we will] give a large number of men employment at good wages."[8]

A Note on Mission Statements

Sometimes the terms, *mission* statement and *vision* statements, are used interchangeably, but they should be written differently, and are intended for different audiences. *Vision* statements are **internal** statements that motivate and inspire employees of an organization to work toward an aspirational vividly described future goal that is 20–30 years out. *Mission* statements are **external** statements shared outside the organization to show new or potential customers, and new or potential investors, what makes the organization unique, whom they serve, what their current goals are, how they contribute, and what sets them apart today.

Triune Brain Theory

So now you know what some of the industry leaders, who have consistently outperformed the market, have done to communicate their vision and successfully influence, inspire, and generate leadership results. How would you like ***extraordinary results*** in not only communicating a vision but in ensuring that it is quickly and wholeheartedly adopted? Let's go back to the research, specifically advancements in neurosciences and how the brain is influenced in decision making.

We often describe ourselves as informed decision makers who think, rationalize, and analyze before making a decision, but it might surprise you to know just how little our decisions are impacted by our *rational thoughts* and the data presented to support them. We like to *think* that we are making decisions leveraging logical centers of the brain, but neuroscience suggests that we make decisions leveraging emotional centers of the brain primarily, and then rationalize our already made decision, using the data we have been given. The brain processes information in three centers before making a decision, and if you want to better influence someone's thought process, and the adoption of your vision, it pays to understand how the brain works and how to present information more successfully.

Paul D. MacLean was an American physician and neuroscientist who first popularized the Triune Brain Theory, which categorized the brain into the three distinct parts below:

The **reptilian brain,** the oldest part of the brain, which evolved first, is found in all animals, and includes the brainstem and cerebellum. It controls the body's core functions like heart rate, breathing, and balance. It's the part of the brain that is instinctual and responsible for assessing danger and the appropriate fight or flight response to ensure our survival. It's also the most impulsive part of the brain, which consistently seeks basic essentials for the sustainment of life, such as food, reproduction, and safety.

The **limbic brain** evolved next, is found in all mammals, and includes the hippocampus, the amygdala, and the hypothalamus. This part of the brain records memories of behaviors that produced pleasant or unpleasant past experiences. This part of the brain is responsible for your emotions and value judgements. The limbic system is where mostly unconscious value judgments are made, which strongly impact our behavior and has no capacity for language.

The **neocortex** part of the brain evolved most recently, is found only in humans, and includes the neocortex and two large cerebral hemispheres with almost infinite learning abilities. This is the part of the brain that *thinks* and is responsible for creativity, complex thinking, logic, our ability to analyze, language, abstract thought, imagination, and consciousness.

The Path to Influencing a Decision

Neuroscientist, Dr. Joseph LeDoux, states that our brain waves flow from the **oldest** to the **newest** parts of our brains when making a decision.[9] This means that an assessment of danger, trust, and survival happens in the reptilian brain; then emotional feelings and value judgements happen in the limbic brain, all before rationalizing, and language is processed in the neocortex brain. So, if you want to influence someone's thinking, and get them to embrace your vision, you need to address all three areas of the brain, and in the most influential order.

To get someone to adopt your vision, you need to first get by the reptilian brain that aims to keep this person safe from harm. You need to establish trust before they (really) consider anything you're saying. If you were paying attention to the third step, *Establishing Trust*, in our *Five Steps to Influence and Inspire Extraordinary Results™*, you already have this well in hand, and you can move to the next area of the brain, the limbic brain. Processing in the limbic brain happens seemingly automatically, as it consults memories of past experiences really quickly; so quickly, it is said that the *feeling* limbic brain is 200 times faster than the *thinking* neocortex brain.[10] Here is where the rubber hits the road. You need to tap into those past experiences and the emotions they generate in order to get people to adopt your vision. While you were in step one, *Making a Connection*, you likely uncovered a lot about what was important to this person or audience, what they are passionate about, and what motivates them as you listened and inquired at level three listening. You need to use these to tap into the emotions of your target audience. Here's why: Neuroscience says that the reptilian brain, which makes decisions to ensure survival, and the super-fast emotional limbic brain, account for 95% of the final decision! That means that our most recently evolved *thinking* neocortex is not only the last one to the decision party; it only accounts for 5% of the final decision. If in your attempt to persuade others, you focus on presenting vast amounts of data and numbers to persuade people to your vision, your data only appeals to the neocortex, and you're in some trouble. That said, your numbers are still important because it's what individuals use to save face and rationalize their decision in the neocortex that was already made in a fraction of the time by the rest of the brain. Ultimately, neuroscience research suggests that reason and logic do not persuade; they merely back up an emotionally made decision.

Influencing 95% of the Decision

Remember, the reptilian brain is primal, so "KISS" (keep it simple stupid) applies. Our lives grow increasingly more complex with vast amounts of people, media, and devices demanding our attention, so keep it simple to break through the noise. Don't make someone work to understand your vision. Concepts, such as intergraded approach, flexible solutions, across all verticals, etc., are less effective.

Tap into the older brain's emotional persuasion. If you don't, your *request for decision* will not go to the limbic brain for a fast, emotionally based decision, which taps into the lifelong database of past pleasant and unpleasant experiences. Instead, your request will be forwarded to the neocortex brain for a lengthy, contemplating, critiquing, option weighing, time consuming, and cognitive evaluation.

The old brain is self-focused/self-centered, and survival is a selfish instinct. That means your vision has to include the person you are speaking to. They should be in the center of the picture you paint of that aspirational future. They need to know what's in it for them, what role they will play, etc. The vision will have benefits for communities, target markets, etc., of course, but if you want to keep this person's older brain interested, you have to appeal to its basic self-interests.

How Do You Do That?

You can access and influence the older brain via emotional persuasion that conveys empowerment and security by playing to its preferences for feelings of comfort, control, acceptance, power, freedom, love, etc. The older brain likes contrast: before/after, higher/lower, more money/less money, fast/slow, with/without, etc. Hence, avoid gray areas in shared information. The older brain better remembers beginnings and endings. This is why some performers like to be first or last on stage during a competition, as intuition and experience has taught them that these are the performances the audience best remember. This is also why the communication pieces we develop for clients highlight important content up front and at the end as part of a communication strategy to ensure that it's remembered. The older brain loves the familiar, so if you can tap into well-known stories or shared experiences, the brain will use them to access stored information or belief paradigms, and make assumptions to increase decision-making speed. Finally, the older brain is visual. The saying, "A picture is worth a thousand words," really does speak to the balance that each contributes to decision making (the neocortex processes language and only contributes 5% of the decision). Include images that support your *aspirational, future-focussed, vividly described vision,* where possible.

With Great Knowledge Comes Great Responsibility

The marketing world has been leveraging many of these processes and tactics to better influence consumer purchasing decisions for years. Consumers aren't always buying from the best manufacturer, but instead buy from companies with whom they connect with on some emotional level, filling an emotional need. For example, *belonging* to a community or being *dominant* among competitive peers with the latest technology, created by those who *think different* and don't follow the masses. There's been some criticism since the first piece of research was published, in 2004, by Read Montagne,

Professor of Neuroscience at Baylor College of Medicine, on what science has dubbed *neuromarketing*. Some have suggested that leveraging the inner brain's workings to influence consumer purchasing decisions is unethical and not unlike subliminal advertising. Of course, subliminal advertising has been banned but neuromarketing, seems here to stay. Remember, research tells us what your mother or grade school teacher told you: "The limbic brain is only attracted to truly authentic and empathetically shared information."[11] Okay, maybe your mother or teacher didn't use those exact words. If you are dishonest or insincere with how you present your vision statement, you will revert back to step two of our *Five Steps to Influence and Inspire Extraordinary Results*[TM], having lost your target audiences' trust. That is, you will be back to *Building a Relationship*, and it may no longer be the relationship you aspired to create. The information and the researched process I created is not intended to be a system of manipulation, but rather awareness to the neuroscience of the brain that empowers leaders with insights as to how best to engage others and present valid information in such a way that it better resonates with its target audience. Knowledge is power. Take the high road when embracing the inner workings of the brain, and do the work to authentically and empathetically communicate the legitimate "what's in it for *them*," through your aspirational, future-state, vividly described vision.

You're not done yet. You may have your target audience on board with the vision, but you need your target audience to buy-in to the mission and the work that needs to be done *today*, to bring the vision of *tomorrow* to fruition. That is step five of the *Five Steps to Influence and Inspire Extraordinary Results*[TM], *Creating Buy-in,* and it's also the subject of our next chapter.

Reflection Pages

What ideas do I want to spend more time reflecting on, and how do they apply to me?

What can I do differently at work, home, or in the communities I serve, to help me grow and demonstrate my leadership?

Why am I doing this?

What does success look like after implementing these changes?

What is my target date to achieve that success?

What steps do I need to take in order to make these changes a reality?

What obstacles do I anticipate?

What resources will I need in people, services, tools, etc. in order to be successful?

How will I hold myself accountable to change and to my timeline?

Who will support me to ensure that what I imagine for myself becomes a reality?

Notes:

1   Collins J, Porras Jl. Building Your Company's Vision: hbr.org: Harvard Business Review; 1996
2   Ibid.
3   Ibid.
4   Ibid.
5   Ibid.
6   Ibid.
6   Ibid.
7   Ibid.
8   Wahid N. I feel, therefore I buy: How your users make buying decisions. Widerfunnel.com: widerfunnel; 2018
9   Kuehn K. The limbic system, the cognitive mind and the user illusion that misleads. Smartcompany.au: smartcompany; 2013
10 Pinay H. Create Loyal Customers For Life: Making Limbic Connections With Experiential Branding. Forbes.org: Forbes Coaches Council; 2017.

Chapter Nine

Creating Buy-In

"In all our associations; in all our agreements let us never lose sight of this fundamental maxim – That all power was originally lodged in, and consequently is derived from, the people."
– George Mason (American patriot; participated in the American Revolution; influential in penning the Bill of Rights)

"Unless both sides win, no agreement can be permanent."
– Jimmy Carter (Former president of the United States, and Nobel Peace Prize recipient)

Five Steps to Influence and
Inspire Extraordinary Results™

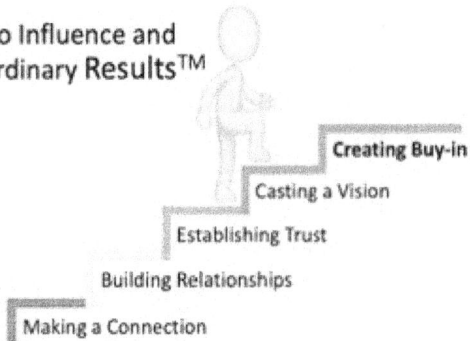

Creating Buy-In

Casting a Vision

Establishing Trust

Building Relationships

Making a Connection

You have an amazing, aspirational, future-focussed, vividly described vision that captures your group's core values and purpose. The vision appeals strongly to your target audience because you took the time to deliver the content in a way that best resonates with how the brain has evolved, and its ability to process information. It's compelling, but how do you get people to buy-in and commit to the work that needs to be done today, to manifest the vision so far into tomorrow?

I Feel You

Indeed, in this fifth and final step of the *Five Steps to Influence and Inspire Extraordinary Results*™, there are some overlaps between casting a vision and creating buy-in, given that a vision is a longer-term goal that includes core ideology, and creating buy-in is about gathering support to deliver on shorter-term goals. Both are goals that benefit from leveraging the neuroscience of how information is processed, suggesting that you should tap into the emotional aspect of any call to action first, before laying on the supporting statistics and data. John P. Kotter is a leading authority on change management, former Harvard Business School professor, and a *New York Times* best-selling author, whose research indicates, "People change what they do, less because they are given analysis that shifts their thinking... [and more] because they are shown a truth that influences their feelings... behavior change happens in highly successful situations, mostly by speaking to people's feelings. This is true even in organizations that are very focussed on analysis and qualitative measurement, even among people who think of themselves as smart in an M.B.A. sense."[1] Planning your execution can make all the difference between an initiative that is well supported, versus one that is merely tolerated or fails miserably. An initiative that is merely tolerated, or is an actual failure, taxes morale, spoils effort, and incurs unproductive expense. Unfortunately, research shows that "70% of all organizational change efforts fail."[2]

Anxiety Around Change

The only thing that never changes is continuous change. Despite its prevalence, people still respond emotionally to change with anxiety, for a number of reasons. Individuals are afraid of the unknown versus the comfort of the status quo. They can fear losing their status or control of their agenda. They fear increased workloads, new working relationships, and not being able to manage new responsibilities or technologies proficiently. This may also cause frustration and the fear of looking inept in front of peers.

So, what can you do as a leader of a team or individual leader among collaborating peers to overcome these obstacles today, to ensure that your vision, or the organization's vision, manifests in a future tomorrow?

Vision Alignment

Ensure that your mission and subsequent call to action aligns with your shared vision. Your messaging should answer these questions and convey the following: How does today's mission, or what you need the team to do today, support your vision? That is, your shared core values, core purpose, and vividly described, big, hairy, audacious goal. Where are you today against your vision? What tangible and realistic targets need to be achieved today in order to move the group closer to that vision? How can the team do this? Create a sense of excitement that is positive, hopeful, and inclusive of your target audience. Convey confidence in the team's ability to pull together and rise to the challenge. Everyone should hold a picture in their mind of what the team aims to achieve, and how this initiative will bring them closer to it.

Create a Sense of Urgency

Why do you *have to* do this? What is happening in the marketplace, or what is the competition doing that demands action to stay competitive or continue to lead? What technologies or processes are being phased out, or are slowing you down, that need to be replaced or risk being left behind? Do more than appeal to the neocortex with statistics and numbers; engage the older brain with a compelling story of what could be lost if such threats aren't addressed, or what dominance could be gained if opportunities are timely seized.

Tell a Story

Your story should acknowledge any negative emotions being felt by your target audience, which you anticipated after doing some initial homework and pulse taking. Your story should also put many of those negative emotions at ease by sharing case studies, or other examples, that demonstrate other companies taking similar action and being rewarded for doing so.

Everyone's Favorite Radio Station: WIIFM

"The vision sounds great, and I feel really good about what we're doing, but I may never see it come to fruition, so if I contribute today, WIIFM, what's in it for me?" Those tangible and realistic targets need to be relevant and relatable to your target audience. That means demonstrating how supporting the plan will help them personally. Above and beyond the satisfaction of fulfilling one's purpose and altruistic contributions, our attention and interests are usually focussed on two limited resources, which we hold in high regard: time and money. You should share your projections on how much money this initiative will save, what could be done with the funds elsewhere in the organization, etc. How much capacity will be saved with the changes? Where could this capacity or productivity be better invested so that everyone benefits, etc.?

I Need Your Help with This

"I have some thoughts and ideas about what we could achieve together. I realize it's strongly influenced by my personal point of view. I would appreciate your input on how we can move forward on this and make the plan a stronger one, with your input. What am I missing? What would you do differently? How can we make this work more effectively?" These are some questions you can ask to prompt engagement and input into your plan of action. There is a good chance that you overlooked something. You'll benefit from collecting additional perspective and insights that you may not be aware of. Research indicates that leaders who ask for advice are seen as more credible, as it demonstrates your commitment to get the details right, and that your opinion is an informed one.[3] Your envisioned end state should be your goal, and provided team recommendations aren't cost prohibitive or inefficient, it would serve you well to demonstrate some flexibility in adapting your plan to include the team's perspectives. In this way, "the plan" becomes "our plan," and the ownership, commitment, and buy-in is enhanced. Many—my less educated self included—focus on selling, not creating buy-in. That is, we sell our ideas to others, prepare for any questions, and "sell them" on our plan. The plan might be supported with solid numbers, process summaries, manual references, screen shots addressing anticipated inquiries, and current policies being honored, but most individuals like to feel that they contributed, and that they were included, before they whole heartedly buy-in and pitch in. Some even work to sabotage or slow down initiatives, despite the benefits to the organization, because they didn't feel sufficiently included. Hence, doing the work to be inclusive may slow things down initially, but you'll pick up speed and commitment from the team later because you made the effort.

Strategic Advocates and Centers of Influence

Depending on the dynamics of the team you're working with, it may be productive to strategically reach out in advance to individuals across the organization, who can help you create buy-in for your plan. You should be strategic, both in terms of the areas or departments you approach, and the specific people in them. You might be working on enhancing an online customer application for investment purchasing; hence, it would be appropriate to have key stakeholders, like IT, customer experience advocates, regulatory compliance overseers, members of the sales team, and the product manager, etc., at the table. If you have a choice, it's important to select people who have influence via their leadership skills, most importantly; then expertise, and then individuals who borrow influence from their title. You might be surprised by whose name pops up as a natural influencer. For this reason, it's important to include different levels of individuals. Create an "influence sandwich," where individuals at the top of the hierarchy, and individual front liners, each contribute to your idea and become advocates to help establish buy-in with the masses. Each lend unique perspective, have unique objections, and will help you establish powerful responses to future questions that will likely be asked by others. As advocates, they will not only help you manage the change; they'll help you lead it in word and action. Meet regularly to keep everyone up to speed with where you are at, but efficiently, to respect each member's time. If it's a longer project, consider having *terms*, where individuals lend their time and expertise for a set amount of time or *term*, before rotating someone else in. This prevents overburdening contributors, keeps the group's energy up for the long haul, and is a source of ongoing fresh ideas. Don't forget to publicly acknowledge the original and existing group members for their contributions whenever you can, appropriately and authentically.

Communication Strategy

Your communication strategy will vary depending on who your target audience is and how complicated the pending changes are, etc. As a former communication consultant to business lines in a large Canadian organization, having an internal audience of 60,000 plus, I can tell you it's important to find ways to creatively repeat your message in varying formats. This ensures that people get the information they need in order to be successful at implementing your plan or the changes you are proposing, and it acknowledges the research that indicates people need to hear the same message a number of times before it's committed to memory. Your message is competing with every other message your target audience is struggling to absorb. The sheer volumes of messages and commitments to other attention hoarding priorities will test their attention bandwidth. Also, different individuals have different preferences for learning mediums. It's important to vary the mediums by including some interactive formats, keeping it fresh, and brief, where possible. Remember, the easier it is for people to understand what you want from them, the easier it will be for them to comply and become advocates for your easy to remember and easy to repeat message. Videos, memos, spaced email drips, meetings, town halls, road shows, intranet news, online interactive learning/testing, dedicated support lines, live chat, closed chat rooms, social media, webinars, podcasts, etc. are all options. Where creativity abounds, so do available options.

Remember to leverage how 95% of decisions are processed in the brain. Respect the neuroscience and avoid the temptation to be all facts and figures, which engages the language processing neocortex who joins the decision-making party later, mostly to justify the decision that the limbic brain already made 200 times faster based on emotions and referencing past experiences. For example, you can include a note from an influential and admired person, or a short video that is inspirational and conversational in tone, preferably as a preamble to more metrics-based content, to accomplish this.

Create different length versions of a story that speaks to what the changes are, why they are important for us, and what the required call to action is. This way, you're prepared for a one-minute elevator ride, longer coffee meetings, or even longer round table discussions with detail favoring audiences.

Whether you're aiming to influence a team of six or 60,000, there will always be naysayers who bring the valuable quality of skepticism. These individual's comments and questions only make your proposals stronger, as they highlight unaddressed or poorly communicated aspects of your initiative. Rumors and gossip often fill gaps in communication, like weeds in a sparsely grassed yard. On rare occasions, regardless of what you share, and every genuine effort you make, there are individuals who will inevitably take exception to one thing or another. You may have to call this person out or help them seek different opportunities that better align with their rigid or strongly contrasting views. Individuals like these can sideline initiatives, as they sabotage positive momentum building and the buy-in of other team members. Don't fool yourself into thinking that the saboteur is always the quiet supporting role who's a chronic complainer. Sometimes the circle going into the square is a senior contributor who doesn't share the organization's culture of ongoing improvement or passionate commitment to lead in the industry, etc. Failing to deal with this interference can come back to haunt you, in a *holy terror* kind of way, not like a *toothpaste mark that keeps appearing on your shirt as it dries* kind of way. Worse yet, they will deprive the others and the organization of the benefits of the initiative and any additional success it supports.

Set People up for Success

As suggested previously, consider assigning tasks based on people's strengths, to better ensure their success by playing to those strengths. Research shows us that this not only improves employee engagement but also sustains contributor's interests and feelings of accomplishment. Again, allow contributors the flexibility to participate in areas that hold their interests, where there is familiarity with the topic, or where there are development opportunities that the experience will provide while communicating clear expectations, measures of success, and accountability.

Train individuals to ensure that they have the required skills or knowledge to be successful. This is really important for train the trainer or support type roles in an organization who become the face of any initiative for others looking for help. Misinformation or wavering in confidence can discourage confidence, not only in the support person but in the soundness of the initiative as well.

Your ability to create buy-in could be vastly improved by simplifying what might seem overwhelming to your team or collaborating peers. Consider breaking larger initiatives into smaller steps. There are a number of benefits to this implementation strategy. The smaller steps require people to learn less information per step; hence, it's easier to digest and *buy-in* to the plan. Anyone who is fearful of the larger change might take comfort in knowing that changes will happen incrementally. This allows the team the opportunity to course correct on smaller aspects of the initiative if required, while protecting the larger whole. Often, lessons learned in initial steps can be applied in subsequent ones that save time and money. Finally, the completion of each step triggers the release of the feel-good chemical, dopamine, in the brain, which we discussed previously. This in itself will reward and motivate contributors to complete more and more steps, to generate more and more feel good dopamine. When potentially overwhelming initiatives are broken down into smaller steps that are successfully implemented, one success builds on the last, positive momentum is created, and buy-in grows stronger and stronger.

Sustainment

Once you've got buy-in, you have to work to keep it! Sustaining the momentum is a lot easier than getting things going initially, but it still requires commitment and effort to ensure that the buy-in for your initiative or mission doesn't start to dwindle.

Once the ball gets rolling on your initiative, unexpected hurdles are bound to surface, or people will start to forget what the short-term objective was and how it supports the organization's longer-term vision. It's important to stay in touch with everyone on different scales. You might meet more frequently with key players, for example. You might make yourself available at certain times of the day, week, or month to lend support. You could set up a specific email or online platform to collect concerns, ideas, and questions, etc. to ensure that people stay informed and engaged, and that buy-in is sustained.

Find opportunities to celebrate! Rig the occasion. Start implementing smaller steps, or identify smaller milestones in the larger plan, so that you are guaranteed a win and a motivating celebration. This will create stronger buy-in as success after success starts to build. Take the time to carve out the right steps or milestones. Undoubtedly, there will be setbacks. If you can, keep the more labor intensive or more expensive steps for later, so that critics have less to gripe about should one of the initial steps not fare as well, and until momentum has been established. Encourage a spirit of continuous improvement, where challenges are not only expected, they're welcomed, because each one survived makes you stronger.

Finally, in everything you do, you need to walk the talk. Nothing influences, inspires, and generates extraordinary results like leading in words, and more importantly, in action. When the team you lead, or the group of individual leaders you collaborate with buy-in, your plan or initiative is less dependent on your energy to keep it going. Instead, it starts to leverage the group's energy that you helped create.

Reflection Pages

What ideas do I want to spend more time reflecting on, and how do they apply to me?

What can I do differently at work, home, or in the communities I serve, to help me grow and demonstrate my leadership?

Why am I doing this?

What does success look like after implementing these changes?

What is my target date to achieve that success?

What steps do I need to take in order to make these changes a reality?

What obstacles do I anticipate?

What resources will I need in people, services, tools, etc. in order to be successful?

How will I hold myself accountable to change and to my timeline?

Who will support me to ensure that what I imagine for myself becomes a reality?

Notes:

1   Martinuzzi, B. 9 Ways To Get Others To Buy In On Change, Americanexpress.com: American Express Business Trends and Insights; 2013.
2   Hedges, K, How To Get Real Buy-In For Your Idea. Forbes.com: Forbes; 2015.
3   Ibid.

Chapter Ten
Case Study – Launching a New Online Customer Tool

"It's important to have a sound idea,
but the really important thing is the implementation."
– Wilbur Ross (United States Secretary of Commerce)

"The best big idea is only going to be as good as its
implementation."
(Jay Samit – American Digital Media Innovator,
Independent Vice Chairman of Deloitte)

In the following case study, italics will be used to call out trends, research, and concepts discussed in previous chapters, which support or are part of the *Five Steps to Influence and Inspire Extraordinary Results*™. Thomas, our main character, will be implementing these steps to generate extraordinary results as a leader among collaborating peers.

Background

Thomas and his peers are working together to build a tool that allows customers to purchase investments online. Thomas is an IT specialist on a newly formed *agile* team, having other *subject matter experts* in marketing, regulatory compliance, customer experience, the investment product group, learning and performance, and someone at the overseas contact center, who will be supervising the customer support group. They all work for the same organization, but only two of them know each other, and some new outside faces will be joining them for the initiative. These unknown individuals just got this *temporary gig* and are outside consultants who will contribute as a project manager, copy writer, graphic artist, and direct marketing specialist. They're all very *different personalities*, some very charismatic and free spirited, while others seem very organized and serious. All are excited to be part of this important project.

The team has a small, 4-week window, or *sprint*, to get the first phase of their project done. There's a lot to do, and little room for error. This is the second time the organization is trying to pull this together. The organization has undergone some *restructuring* and, as a result of *delayering*, they lost contributors who had useful knowledge from past experiences and insights into *where in the organization their ideas often got stuck.* Thomas heard that the previous IT solution put forth "missed the mark," and despite the time already invested, and months of expense, the order of the day was to start from scratch with the newly invited names copied on his email.

Most of his peers on the team are younger *millennials*. Thomas has heard a lot about millennials—what they are like and why they do what they do. He has met lots of millennials who *don't fit the mold,* and finds that the reasons why they do things are often misunderstood. He has decided to meet these new peers with a *curious open mind, and suspend any judgement,* good or bad.

Thomas is the most senior person on his team, having been around for over a decade, when many of the others were still in school. He's been working with a *performance coach to better influence, inspire, and generate extraordinary results* when working in *collaborative teams,* and he's eager to try some of the suggestions and tactics he's been practicing over the last six months. Thomas wants to improve *his effectiveness,* and help this initiative meet with *greater success* the second time round. He wants to show everyone, especially his boss, that he has grown and is an *effective leader* who can *influence, inspire, and generate extraordinary results in collaborative environments.* He knows the world is always changing, and it's impossible to predict the future or control hiring and firing trends, but he wants to do what he can to feel more secure in his career, as many colleagues have since left the organization, some on their own accord, and some not. This initiative will be the perfect opportunity to showcase his enhanced skills and the value he adds to this team and the organization. If nothing else, the skills he practices here will help him close what *LinkedIn's CEO, Jeff Weiner, announced was the biggest skill gap on résumés in 2019—soft skills, specifically leadership, communication, and teambuilding.*

He suspects that all these *subject matter experts* really know their stuff, and that brings him some comfort, but he also knows they're going to have to tap into an entirely different set of soft skills, which have nothing to do with their expertise, in order to be successful. The organization really needs this to go well, as the competition has already gone to market with their version of an online investment purchasing tool, which is getting a lot of media attention. Thomas wants this win for the organization, but he also wants *anything with his name on it to be a success.*

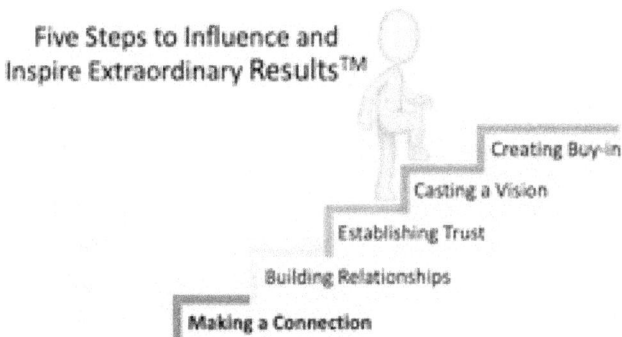

Five Steps to Influence and
Inspire Extraordinary Results™

Creating Buy-in

Casting a Vision

Establishing Trust

Building Relationships

Making a Connection

Making a Connection

Thomas logged into the team's first conference call, which included *remote contributors* that were overseas, as well as *consultants* working in neighboring countries. It was all pretty standard: review timelines, project charter, statement of work, etc. Thomas thought that the project manager did a good job on the call, but it feels like the team is already slow out of the gate. He knows this is a very competent, expensive team of professionals, but it feels like he's in a sports car with the emergency brake still on. Being the IT *subject matter expert*, he knows he's a key contributor in developing this application. He decides to step up his *leadership and influence via his communication and collaboration techniques,* to ensure that he and the team meet with *extraordinary results*. Thomas was doing his best to *listen at a leadership level three*. He didn't *interrupt, nodded*, and even *repeated back statements* to ensure that he heard them correctly, and to convey he was *listening.* Thomas felt a little strange asking some *open-ended questions*, but he nonetheless asked what seemed on the surface to be an obvious question. He wanted to *check for understanding,* and this was a crucial starting point for communicating clear expectations. He asked, "What does the ultimate customer experience look like when using this new online tool?" To his and the others' surprise, everyone had differing responses to the same question. IT thought it was the speed of the transaction (get the customer in and out asap); compliance wanted to ensure that the customer had all the legal disclosures up front, to ensure customers were aware of the risks in investing online, before moving forward. The product people wanted the customer to immediately see product information, like benefits and features, so that customers would be more inclined to make a purchase. The marketing people spoke of photos that communicated the emotional feelings that a customer would feel in their future life if they purchased the product today. The marketers used words like *comfortable, control your life, security, freedom*, etc., and were not keen on feature lists at all. There was a flurry of heated discussion, and while it took some time, Thomas was glad that he *didn't just listen and make assumptions* about what each member meant. He tried hard to *stay open, and to be likable, humble, and adaptable.* When the conversation came to a bit of *an impasse,* Thomas reminded the group that they *shared many emotional feelings* and goals coming into this process, like wanting to do well individually, wanting to be understood by the others, being appreciative for any additional clarity others brought or elicited from the group, etc. This helped them feel like they already had something *in common,* and it helped *connect* them. By asking additional *open and closed ended questions to confirm his understanding,* Thomas brought the solutions manufacturing team closer to a shared understanding of what was being built, and made them feel more *connected* as a group.

Before signing off the call, Thomas suggested the idea of setting up a team profile on an internal web page, where each team member could answer 4–5 questions about themselves, including some interesting facts about them outside work, like hobbies and places travelled. The group loved the idea and agreed to review the profiles together on the next call. Sarah, the project manager, suggested they recap highlights of the project there, and use the portal to post links to updated project related documents instead of emailing them constantly. Thomas also suggested reviewing their *aspirational, future focussed, vividly described vision* of what the organization was working toward, and discussing how this project's *mission* will contribute toward that future vision. This way, the *diverse group* could feel like they were on *common ground* in terms of what they were working toward. Thomas felt this would help acknowledge that each member was *unique, but united in their cause.* The group was very receptive to the idea, and it was agreed that Thomas would take the lead on this during their next call.

After the video conference call, Thomas decided to watch the recorded call, and he noticed that he was only one of two people standing on screen. He did this purposefully to ensure that as much of his *physiology* was on camera as possible. He remembered his workshop that spoke to Dr. Mehrabian's *7-35-55 rule of personal communication*. That is, the *emotional meaning* of any communication is conveyed via *7% words, 35% voice tonality, and 55% body language*. He wanted to ensure that he was in full view of his audience so that they could see his *raised open hands, eye contact, and enthusiastic gestures.* He was also keen to watch the recording because he and his coach had both agreed, after watching his last meeting, that he spent a lot of time with his head down, reading his notes and preparing to raise his next point, instead of making *eye contact, nodding, repeating back, or asking questions*. Both he and his coach agreed that he was not conveying interest in what the speaker was saying, or demonstrating that he was actually *listening.*

Thomas has been really focussed on his *personal development*. Before this year, he never even spoke of *emotional intelligence*. This year, he and his coach are working on implementing and bringing to life his new knowledge in the areas of *emotional self-awareness, self-regulation, motivation, empathy, and social skills* that he learned about in a recent workshop. He finds himself thinking about that group conference call. He doesn't feel like he has achieved that important first step of *Making a Connection,* in the *Five Steps to Influence and Inspire Extraordinary* Results*TM. He's* optimistic this will change during the next call, when they have some fun reviewing their profiles, the organization's *vision,* and the project's *mission statement.*

Listening to his overseas collaborators, Thomas can relate to the struggle to express one's self sometimes, when English isn't your first language. That said, Thomas decided to exercise some *discretionary effort,* and reached out to the contact center lead, Aarav, for a more personal call, and to demonstrate part of his *emotional intelligence, empathy*. Thomas was new to Canada, 15 years ago. English was not his first language, and *he could personally relate* to what his contact center colleague was feeling while communicating with the others. Thomas asked a few *non-work-related,* polite questions, such as, *"How is life outside work?"* and, *"Do you have any hobbies that you enjoy?"*

Thomas also offered to be a resource to his contact center peer, should he need to bounce ideas off anyone. Fifteen minutes later, the two were laughing after discovering they both have two older daughters that test their sanity on a regular basis. Aarav is happy that Thomas took the *time* and made the *effort* to call him, as he feels much more *connected* to Thomas. Before they hung up, they wished each other well until their next virtual call.

Thomas will make good on his commitment to develop the shared internal portal, and the team will really appreciate his *discretionary effort,* as *effort expressed in action, speaks louder than any words.* They also appreciate his work ethic and commitment to their mutual success. More and more, the team is starting to like Thomas, feel a stronger connection to each other, and are looking forward to *having a little fun outside their regular routine.*

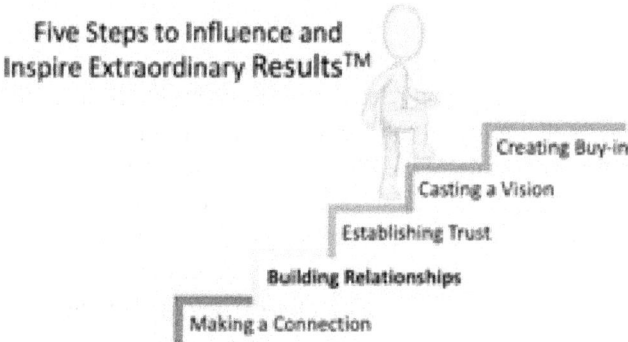

Five Steps to Influence and
Inspire Extraordinary Results™

Creating Buy-in

Casting a Vision

Establishing Trust

Building Relationships

Making a Connection

Building Relationships

Thomas has always been sociable and has embraced a *childlike curiosity* about everyone he meets. He *genuinely takes interest in others and understanding their unique talents.* Thomas encouraged others to talk about themselves after attending a keynote that spoke to the importance of relationship building. He remembered hearing about *happy feelings* generated by the production of *dopamine in the brain* as one *speaks of themselves* to an *audience,* and how the speaker then attributes those happy feelings to the listener who helped create them. While on camera, Thomas smiled a *Duchenne smile,* engaging both the muscles around his mouth and eyes. He marveled at the accuracy of the research, which predicts that the *speaker will adopt his smile as the speaker subconsciously checks the validity* of Thomas's smile!

Thomas surprised everyone by using *individual names in conversation* whenever he directed a question that was specific to someone in the group. The person being asked the question felt so *welcomed and honored* to have this man, whom they had only just met, use their name so confidently. It made them feel like they already *had a relationship* even though they had just met. The others all wondered how he knew all their *names,* and how he could seem so comfortable. Thomas did his homework. At a planning session with his performance coach, Thomas *was committed* and crafted a strategy to help him learn the group members' names. Thomas took a screen shot of the group, as their faces were displayed in his computer's conference call application. He printed that screen shot and carefully *paid attention* and listened as individuals announced themselves, then wrote their names on their pictures. Before every call, Thomas reviewed the pictures until he could list off every name accurately without reading the names. It took a little bit of effort, but every member he addressed personally, felt like they had a *relationship* with him.

One of the team members *thanked Thomas for his effort* in building the internal portal, and *soon, several of the others were doing the same*. Thomas also found himself giving *authentic* and *specific* praise for a job well done. It appears that there's truth to the research that says *showing gratitude perpetuates a spirit of gratitude and a pay-it-forward mentality* that could change the culture of an organization. The pleasure inducing effects of a *dopamine release were felt by both the individual giving the appreciation or gratitude, and by those receiving it.* Hence, the *givers and receivers of appreciation felt good and were soon motivated to give out more and more appreciation, in a virtuous cycle,* to generate more and more *dopamine releases/rewards.*

Thomas smiled as he watched some of the younger members update the others in some non-traditional ways, leveraging the latest in presentation tricks, and he held his tongue. As long as they were *on time and on budget,* he wasn't going to encourage them to do it any differently. After all, they should be *playing to their strengths,* not his.

Five Steps to Influence and
Inspire Extraordinary Results™

Creating Buy-in

Casting a Vision

Establishing Trust

Building Relationships

Making a Connection

Establishing Trust

More and more, the team felt *committed* to each other's needs as *certainty or security generated by their reliance on the character, ability, strength, and truth* of each other continued to build as trust bloomed. Thomas had a peek at the notes he took at a recent workshop, for some numbers he thought important enough to write down.

He found the following notes:

Paul J. Zak, American neuroeconomist and Harvard researcher. Lots of accolades, i.e. smart guy/well known in field; invested decades researching the neurological connection between trust, leadership, and organizational performance...

Studied how certain behaviours release "the trust chemical," oxytocin, in the brain, which signals that someone is safe to approach or work with...

Found that "compared with people at low-trust companies, people at high-trust companies report 74% less stress, 106% more energy at work, 50% higher productivity, 13% fewer sick days, 76% more engagement, 29% more satisfaction with their lives, and 40% less burnout."

Thomas wanted *more energy, higher productivity, less stress, and more engagement* for his collaborating peers and himself! What he had to do, according to his notes, was build trust by:

- Acting with transparency and integrity
- Giving trust to get trust
- Recognizing the contributions of others
- Showing vulnerability
- Being altruistic

That seemed like a lot of work, but Thomas wanted the *benefits in health, performance, engagement, and results that trust would bring* to this project. So, he sat down and created a plan to enhance his personal performance, and a strategy to deliberately impact the overall performance of the group by building trust. He came up with the following plan to share with his performance coach at their next session:

To *act with transparency and integrity*, I'm going to:

- *Be open! I'm going to* share information about the project quickly, report what is going well and what could be better, and I'm not going to sugar coat anything.
- *Not tell "harmless fibs,"* as this will make my collaborating *peers scrutinize* what comes out of my mouth more closely in the future, or *dismiss what I say altogether because they think I'm untrustworthy.*

To *give trust in order to get trust*, I'm going to:

- *Convey the trust I have in our executive, my boss, and the rest of the team.*
- Do some due diligence, and after assessing that the team is well-equipped for the task at hand, *I'm going to let them execute on their contributions without micromanaging them!*
- *Let someone else take over* managing parts of our internal portal, and let them have the experience, to demonstrate my trust in them by *sharing the responsibility.*

To *recognize the contributions of others*, I'm going to:

- *Shine a spotlight* on Aarav, and *compliment* him on the quality of scripting he and his team has created for the support team! I will *protect* Aarav by not highlighting the hiccup they had with their content on the site.
- *Never shame or blame* Aarav for the delay in our work due to his team's hiccup; instead, I will *focus on the silver lining*, i.e. what we learned about the system's restrictions and how we're going to enhance the system for future use with live customers—for when its performance really matters!

To show vulnerability, I'm going to:

- Show that this is a *safe place to admit mistakes* and to *learn from them*. I will *get visibility* by speaking in front of the whole group, and I'll tell them that our IT team is responsible for the trouble that Aarav and his team had. *We made some assumptions* based on our experience and resources available to us, which we took for granted. We were wrong to make those assumptions. Even if Aarav didn't follow the pages and pages of instruction we provided, we could have been more diligent in our testing, by doing things that the average user might. I'm going to *own it*, as I feel we contributed negatively also.
- *Ask Aarav and his team to help us*. We need real user feedback on what kinds of media best support them. How much bandwidth do they need, etc.? We could also use some constructive criticism on the value of so much detail in the supporting guide. Maybe its length is discouraging people from getting through it, and is contributing to the challenges…. Maybe we could *be a little more human,* and tone down some of the formality in our content. Given that many of Aarav's team speak English as a second language, we could better communicate the basics without the formal words and jargon…

To be altruistic, I'm going to:

- Generate trust by *giving of my time, energy,* and what I have to offer in terms of skills, without expectations of reward. So, I'm going to offer my support to anyone who wants to help out with maintaining the internal portal. I'll probably spend more time teaching up front than if I had just done these tasks myself, but I know this will demonstrate that I want good things for others. In fact, I'm going to invest in *determining the development goals of others* on our team. I'll ask if anyone has a desire to explore or develop a new expertise for their personal development or résumé, and I'll support them as their coach along the way!

Thomas puts down his pen and feels good about his plan. He knows when trust is present, individuals in *organizations feel safer* knowing that they *can count on each other* to have *the character to do the right thing, and be accountable for their actions without fear. With trust, individuals support each other as they take calculated risks without fear of persecution for making a mistake. With trust comes the absence of fear and uncertainty,* and the much-coveted *innovation, creativity, collaboration, and productivity* that he wants for his collaborating peers.

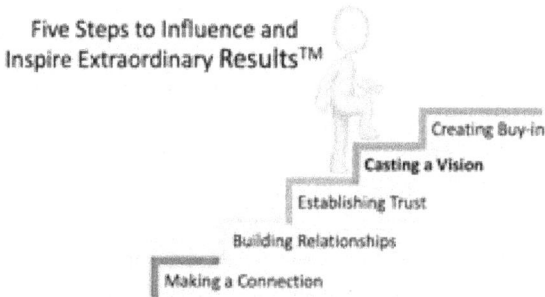

Five Steps to Influence and
Inspire Extraordinary Results™

Creating Buy-in

Casting a Vision

Establishing Trust

Building Relationships

Making a Connection

Casting a Vision

The team met online today. Thomas was excited as he had done a lot of work on their initiative and on his own personal development. He was eager to share the organization's vision statement, and only hoped that he could help the others see just how important it is to everyone in their organization. He thought their CEO did a great job introducing the vision; after she and the special task force invited to create it, were done. It was *compelling,* as well as *inspirational,* and made Thomas *proud* to work for the organization. To him, the vision statement acted as a *beacon* to show the way toward a *vividly described aspirational future.*

As promised, Thomas shared the organization's vision statement with the team. Some of them already knew it, as they worked for the same organization, but he thought it was always a *good idea to review it throughout the year* and keep it fresh in mind, *not just posted on a wall* somewhere. The *outside contractors* joining the team as part of a temporary gig, got real *insight into the character of the organization, what drives them to do what they do, how they do it, and the commitment they demonstrate.*

Thomas posted the organization's vision statement below, to the portal:

We will be guided by integrity, compassion, and customer centricity as we empower our customers with the confidence and stability they deserve, while pursuing today the financial means to create their dreams of tomorrow. With this commitment to our customer, we expect to be one of the most accessible investment dealer firms in the world, where customers can use our services at their convenience, be it at home, while on vacation, while working remotely on the other side of the country, or during retirement in any one of many cities around the world.

Thomas and the team feel that they have a solid business plan for this project, but inspired by the organization's vision statement, they decide to draft their own project *mission statement,* which is a *present-focused statement that supports the organization's future-focused vision statement.* They came up with the following:

Project "Invest Remotely" will provide a secure and efficient way for customers to build the financial resources to make their short and long-term goals a reality, with easy access to robust investment tools, investment options, and meticulously trained customer support.

The team was a little surprised by how *emotional* everyone was feeling after the exercise. Of course, it was exactly what Thomas wanted. Thomas was trying to *generate extraordinary;* that is, he wanted everyone to adopt the organization's vision, and he knew he could do it more effectively by leveraging his knowledge about *how the human brain makes decisions.* He knew he had *three levels of brain* to influence, and that *95% of the decision* was made by the first two levels! He first cleared the *reptilian brain* by demonstrating that this was a safe space, and by introducing ideas about *"what's in it for them."* For example, new learning opportunities, recognition, additions to their résumé, etc. Then Thomas *got past the limbic brain by attaching emotion to the decision,* by sharing the organization's vision and getting commitment to it. He also *shared stories* about how it has served them well, and how it *serves as a beacon* that continues to guide their efforts. He also really focussed on the benefits to the customer, and how any consumer, themselves included, would deserve and appreciate the level of service they're going to provide, while helping to make the customers' dreams come true. All this, before speaking to the statistics and logistics of the initiative. The team resonated with the *picture he painted with words,* and the marketing people were quick to jump in and share some of the actual *happy customer centric photos* that they had started to source for the application; thus, confirming that they were indeed on the same page.

The team bought into the organization's future vision and, together, they created a mission statement that spoke to why they were gathered. Following the *Five Steps to Influence and Inspire Extraordinary Results™* from Thomas's workshop, he knew he had to get the team to *buy-in to the work that needed to get done today, which would support the organization's vision for tomorrow.*

Five Steps to Influence and
Inspire Extraordinary Results™

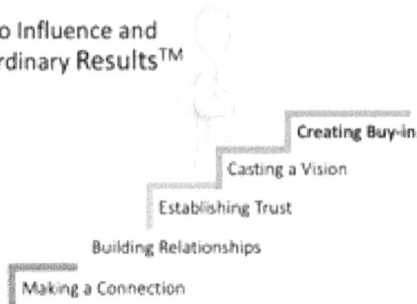

Creating Buy-in

Casting a Vision

Establishing Trust

Building Relationships

Making a Connection

Creating Buy-In

Thomas knew there was some *anxiety* among team members, which he expected given the scope of work and the changes it would require to how their organization currently manages trades. The team loved the organization's vision, but some were expressing *concerns* over the additional *workload*, working with *people they don't know*, losing *control* over how things are done now, and *feeling a little inept* as they won't know how to operate in the new environment initially, much less be able to advocate and encourage others.

Thomas was determined that this time round, this initiative would be completed and have a positive end result that everyone could be proud of. After looking at his workshop notes, he sought some support from his performance coach and, together, they came up with the following plan to generate *buy-in*, the fifth step in the *Five Steps to Influence and Inspire Extraordinary Results™*.

Plan to Create Buy-In:

Vision Alignment

Create a sense of *excitement that is positive, hopeful, inclusive* of the team. *Convey confidence in the team's ability* to pull together and rise to the challenge!

Make sure everyone *holds a picture in their mind* of what the team aims to achieve, and knows *how this initiative will bring them closer to it.*

Create a Sense of Urgency

Remind the group that the competition has already released their online trading application, and it's getting a lot of attention in the media. *If we don't* get ours up and operational, some of our *customers might be lost* to the competition forever, and it will be *harder to sell* our services to new customers who are expecting the convenience as a given.

Tell a Story

Tell the group the story of my friend, Marcus, who works at one of our competitors. He and his colleagues also expressed many of the anxieties we now share, but they stuck with it, and *now they are enjoying the outcome of their efforts.* Their business has improved by 10%, and their customer satisfaction ratings literally became newsworthy as they became first page material for the financial section of the local paper!

WIIFM

Tell the group that Marcus, at the competition, also mentioned how the new processes *saved all kinds of time and money.* Less *time* was required from employees in the back-office processing area and in the supervision of trades. The online format allowed them to *save money* that was reinvested elsewhere by thinning out departments and using those savings to reinvest in departments that supported an excellent customer experience, and invest more in creative marketing to drive more sales.

Ask for help

Ask or say:

- *What am I missing?*
- *What would any of you do differently?*
- *These are my ideas, but I know they're limited to my experience and point of view. I'd be interested to hear how you might do it differently to achieve greater efficiency...*

Thomas writes a quick note to himself, at the corner of his page, to further support buy-in....

* Remember to reach out to the product group, suggest a meeting to talk out some ideas, and ask if Julie might like to join! *

Thomas knows Julie from the investment product department. He also *knows her to be very influential.* Not only would she have great insight from five years of experience in the department, she would be a great *advocate and center of influence* moving forward.

Back on the call, the team agreed that on their next call they would make good headway on a communication strategy. The lead in communication already proposed some innovative and *varied communication mediums* that would be effective at *communicating content and stimulating the audience* to *get their attention* and *keep them engaged.* The lead in communication also volunteered to create *different length stories or scripts* that the team can use in different meetings, from short elevator rides to in-depth meetings, to ensure that there is a *consistent, positive, succinct message that is easy to remember and share.*

Sam, in the learning and performance department, shares some valid points:

- It's apparent that the *before and after state, clearly described,* is considerably different.
- Some kind of *training* needs to be developed to help *set people up for success* and ensure that they have the *skills to perform.*
- If employees struggle later to support other employees or their customers, anxious employees might see the *confusion or lack of information* as a reason to *not support the initiative* or *lose their confidence in the initiative.*
- The confusion might cause anxiety among the organization, and a movement to *revert to old ways!*

Thomas thanks Sam for the input, and asks the team, besides the *training* and a *solid commutation strategy,* what do they think they should do about this? They all agree that they need to map out a *sustainment plan,* one that will have *regular touchpoints* with all those involved, to ensure that people *stay informed and engaged, and that buy-in is sustained.* They agree to divide and reorganize their initiative into *smaller pieces,* and have *easier, less expensive* tasks that will generate *more wins up front.* This should create more opportunities to *celebrate wins,* build *positive momentum,* and *help naysayers gain the confidence* that this team already shares.

The team ends their call with a commitment to a shared pact. Each of them will *walk the talk* and fully acknowledge that while there will be some upsets, each *upset* will be *embraced* in a *spirit of continuous improvement. Challenges will not only be expected but welcomed,* because it will *test our mettle,* and *each problem solved* will *make us stronger.*

Thomas wishes everyone a good night and signs off. He can't stop smiling. The collaborative energy on the team is amazing. He has put quite a bit of work into this initiative already, and a considerable amount of energy into developing his own leadership skills. The initiative is important to the organization, so he's determined to find the energy to make it happen. As for the effort invested in himself, he knows he's influencing and inspiring his collaborating peers to help generate extraordinary results that would otherwise be inaccessible. He also sees the energy put toward personal development as an investment in himself, his future success, and in those who depend on him at work, at home, and in the community he serves. After all, the *"soft" skills he's learning don't have an average half-life of five years like his "hard" skills do.* These *leadership skills are his for life.* While it took some time to review his notes and draw up his plans, his performance coach reminded him that once he got the *Five Steps to Influence and Inspire Extraordinary Results*TM committed to memory, it would become easier and easier to implement, and the rewards would be great.

Thomas already has a new confidence about himself, and is seeing how people are responding more positively around him. Thomas can also see that the focus he placed on enhancing his leadership skills is paying off in saved time for the entire group, and is helping to create a team of positive, collaborative supporters, who are moving mountains with momentum and enthusiasm. Thomas nods to himself as if agreeing with the little voice in his head:

"It's incredible how quickly and effectively initiatives can move forward when the leader of a team, or an individual leader among collaborating peers, can influence and inspire others to generate extraordinary results through enhanced communication and collaboration."

*For support with your transformation, as a growing leader who wishes to influence and inspire others to generate extraordinary results, visit www.embracingleadershift.com for your exclusive access to *The Skills Implementation Planner* and *The Skills Execution Blueprint*. These will help you create an *at a glance* plan of implementation and an *at a glance* execution blueprint. The First resource will encourage you to identify and test different processes and tactics in the book, over time, to see what best resonates with you. The second resource will encourage you to create an execution blueprint, and narrow in on just a handful of skills, that you will aim to incorporate into your Leadership DNA. This will be the "blueprint" of processes and tactics that made your short list and what you plan to consistently use throughout the following year. Remember to use your *Reflection Pages* to help you plan *how* you will complete what you identified in your *at a glance* planning and execution resources.

Wishing you much continued ***extraordinary*** success.

.

About the Author

Ricardo Lopes grew up, and lives, in the Toronto, Canada area with his family. He is an award-winning author, speaker, trainer, and coach serving clients worldwide. He is the founder and managing director of Advanced Leadership, a learning and performance company based in the Toronto area that trains entrepreneurs, educators, corporate leaders, sales professionals, collaborating subject matter experts, and motivated individuals to achieve extraordinary results. Ricardo is uniquely qualified to talk about leadership, given decades of experience in leadership roles in business and corporate world environments, and an almost insatiable appetite for learning and sharing. Ricardo graduated from the University of Toronto and holds an Honours Bachelor of Arts in Sociology and Criminology. Ricardo has studied with the one of the world's most highly ranked and internationally recognized leadership and management development experts, John C. Maxwell, and is an accredited coach and speaker for the John C. Maxwell organization. Ricardo has had many titles, including financial planner, bank manager, sales trainer, communications consultant, national business development coach, and communications specialist, and has helped employees, and clients, become more successful at work, and in life.

The author is available for delivering keynote presentations and workshops, and offering support as a performance coach to appropriate audiences.

For rates and availability, visit www.embracingleadershift.com or email the author at ricardolopes@advancedleadership.ca.

To order additional copies of this book, visit www.amazon.com.

Finally, if you have been inspired by this book to better influence and inspire others to achieve the extraordinary, the best thing you can do is share it! The world is embracing a new culture of leadership, and you can help others not only to embrace the shift in leadership happening around them, but to transform their own leadership, and their life.